DEVELOPMENT

IN   PRACTICE

Better Urban Services

Better Urban Services

Finding the Right Incentives

THE WORLD BANK
WASHINGTON, D.C.

This book is a modified version of a document that was reviewed by the Board
of Executive Directors of the World Bank in September 1994. The book has
benefited greatly from their comments. The volume is a product of the staff of
the World Bank, and the judgments made herein do not necessarily reflect the
view of its Executive Directors or the countries they represent.

*The cover photograph is of Lagos, Nigeria; by Curt Carnemark for the World
Bank.*

Library of Congress Cataloging-in-Publication Data

Better urban services : finding the right incentives
     p.   cm. — (Development in practice)
   Includes bibliographical references.
   ISBN 0-8213-3232-5
   1. Municipal services—Developing countries.   2. Decentralization
in government—Developing countries.   3. Intergovernmental fiscal
relations—Developing countries.   4. World Bank—Developing
countries.   I. Title. II. Series: Development in practice (Washington, D.C.)
   HD4431.D56   1995
   363'.09172'4—dc20   95-17819
                                                             CIP

Contents

Foreword

THIS study comes at a key juncture for the world's urban areas. Urbanization is proceeding rapidly, and it is projected that by the year 2020 more than half the population of the developing world will live in cities and towns. Yet even as cities increasingly become the nexus of economic and population growth, they do not deliver on the promise of a better quality of life to the extent they could. Millions of urban residents do not have potable water near their homes, basic sanitation is often lacking, and access to health services and education pose serious problems in many cities.

Failures in the coverage and quality of urban services in developing countries are the result of more than a lack of resources. The evidence shows that, in many cases, the resources devoted to urban services are substantial but used inefficiently. Therefore, it is essential to look to the system of mobilizing and managing these resources: the institutional arrangements for urban service delivery. Herein lies an important opportunity to face the challenge of rapid urbanization. Over the last several years and for a variety of reasons, the way governments administer delivery of urban services has been reexamined. Of the seventy-five developing countries with populations over 5 million, all but twelve have initiated some form of transfer of power to local governments. At the same time, the role of the private sector in many areas traditionally reserved for government is being reassessed. This fluidity in intergovernmental arrangements and the overall policy environment for local service delivery offer the chance to promote fundamental reforms that would not have been possible in the past.

This book seeks to build a conceptual framework that can help to guide the process of administrative change under way in so many countries. This framework emphasizes looking beyond local governments themselves as the cause of poor performance and seeks to highlight the range of incentives that may determine the quality and responsiveness of local services. These include rules governing fiscal transfers and investment allocation; myriad regulations affecting local government activities; and mechanisms for encouraging government accountability to local constituents, including meaningful participation by the users of services. This conceptual framework draws on a broad evolution of the understanding of institutional performance over the last several years and is firmly grounded in the lessons learned from twenty years of urban lending in the World Bank.

The task of achieving the right mix of incentives to promote better urban service delivery in any given country does not lend itself to universal blueprints or recipes for success. A range of considerations must be balanced to find the appropriate scope, speed, and sequencing of the reform process in a given country. Moreover, it is particularly critical to build broadly based ownership of the reform process in this sensitive area and to encourage inclusive decisionmaking if reforms are to be sustainable.

Although the process of reform will not be simple, the potential payoffs are high. Managing and protecting the urban environment may be either very costly or simply ineffective if the capacity to deliver key urban services such as clean water, sanitation, waste collection, and efficient transport cannot be rapidly expanded in the future. Well-performing, demand-driven urban institutions are critical to this expansion. Strong institutions in urban areas and sound intergovernmental arrangements are critical to the effective management of air and water resources. Finally, if urban services cannot be made more responsive to demands, and financed sustainably, then the evidence suggests that it is the poor who will suffer most from the supply rigidity and implicit rationing that ensue.

This book is a response to an operational challenge facing the Bank, a challenge that has arisen from the needs and interests of the Bank's borrowers as they undergo administrative and political change. It brings together the state of our knowledge and highlights positive new initiatives that should be emulated. It recognizes both opportunities for the future and a number of unanswered questions. As such, it should represent the starting point in a learning process in developing countries, in the Bank, and within the broader external aid and lending community. Originally presented to the World Bank's Board of Executive Directors as a sector review, this revised study is being published to inform the reform processes under way in so many countries, to encourage a broader engagement in the debate of the issues, and to catalyze further learning from the rich experiences of past and future administrative reforms.

Ismail Serageldin
Vice President
Environmentally Sustainable Development
The World Bank

Acknowledgments

THIS book builds on two decades of work by both borrowers and World Bank staff in the field of municipal development. It has drawn extensively on studies by Roy Bahl and Johannes Linn on urban public finance; by Arturo Israel, Eleanor Ostrom, and Samuel Paul on institutional development; and, more recently, by Tim Campbell, Anna Haines, Jerry Silverman, and Don Winkler on decentralization and intergovernmental fiscal relations. A major source of information—both on past practice and on current innovations—has been project officers directly involved in urban lending operations. In addition, the resources of the multiagency, collaborative Urban Management Programme were helpful in the preparation of the book.

The author of the book is Bill Dillinger. The book benefited greatly from the advice of Richard Bird, Ken Davey, and Arturo Israel, from the assistance of the author's colleagues in the Urban Development Division—Fitz Ford, Jim Hicks, Rita Hilton, Jed Kolko, and Victor Vergara—and from the suggestions of other Bank staff, especially in operations. It also benefited from the comments of urban practitioners in several developing countries, whose views were sought throughout the preparation process. The work was carried out under the direction of Louis Y. Pouliquen, Patricia Annez, and Michael Cohen. Alfred Imhoff managed the editorial-production process for the book, and Ding Dizon did the typesetting.

The book is related to earlier policy work in the Transport, Water, and Urban Development Department (TWU) and should be considered in that broader context. The overall framework was laid out by *Urban Policy and Economic Development: An Agenda for the 1990s* (World Bank 1991), which highlighted three main objectives for Bank assistance in urban areas:

alleviating poverty, protecting the urban environment, and enhancing the productivity of economic activities in urban areas. The focus in this work is on strengthening the performance of urban institutions, a key link in raising productivity and obtaining results on the ground. Accordingly, the analysis examines past efforts to develop municipal institutions and factors for improving future performance, including the system of financing, assignments of responsibility across levels of government, and regulations and other incentives affecting local governments.

The book also draws on previous work by TWU (Kessides 1993a) on strategies for delivery of infrastructure services, which has since been incorporated into *World Development Report 1994: Infrastructure for Development* (World Bank 1994). This work developed a framework for examining the respective roles of the public and private sectors in infrastructure delivery and identified means of drawing more effectively on private sector resources to provide the services so essential to well-functioning cities. That work also covered such issues as cost recovery for infrastructure services and management of choices between maintenance and new investment. Accordingly, these topics are covered in far less detail here, although they too are critical to successful municipal development. Moreover, effective institutional arrangements within local governments and across levels of government—the focus of thisbook—provide the framework for achieving a number of these sectoral objectives at the local level.

Overview

THE developing world is being transformed from a world of rural villages into a world of cities and towns. By the year 2020, it is projected that more than half of the population of developing countries will be urban. This demographic shift suggests that cities, in many respects, work. *Urban population growth has been fueled by prospects of higher incomes that have largely been realized. Yet cities do not deliver on the promise of a better quality of life to the extent they could. Despite the relatively higher incomes of urban populations, the quality of services in most cities is poor.* At least 170 million people in urban areas lack a source of potable water near their homes, and the water supplied to those who have access is often polluted. Access to basic sanitation, collection of solid wastes, and urban transport, as well as education and health services, pose similar problems. Increasing violence is adding to the more traditional problems of the quality of life in urban areas. Service failures have implications for the productivity of economic activities in cities; moreover, they typically affect the poor disproportionately.

This book reviews the World Bank's efforts to improve the efficiency and responsiveness of urban service delivery in developing countries. Bank-financed urban projects have typically comprised a mixture of physical investments and measures to strengthen municipal institutional capacity. As highlighted in previous World Bank policy papers, the investment components have been largely quite successful, meeting their physical targets and adding to the availability of shelter and the capacity of municipal infrastructure (World Bank 1993a; unpublished World Bank data). This book pays special attention to the institutional components that are increasingly recognized as essential elements in ensuring the sustainability and replicability of the benefits of the physical investments the Bank supports. *The Bank's initial approach to institutional development (in common with the approach of many other members of the external aid and lending community working in this area) focused on the internal administration of municipal government and relied largely on technical advisory services. A review of experience shows that there are important limits to what can be achieved with this approach. Institutional failures in urban service delivery not only were the result of a lack of technical knowledge on the part of local government staff but also reflected constraints and perverse incentives confronting local personnel and their political leadership.* These, in turn, were often caused by problems in the relationship between central and local governments. Over the past ten to fifteen years, the Bank has increasingly shifted the emphasis toward these issues in its economic and sector work and lending. Based on experience thus far, this book concludes that this shift in emphasis should be accelerated so that, when necessary, reforms of the incentives facing local governments, including intergovernmental institutional arrangements, become a key element in country strategy and project design.

For the Bank and its borrowers, the stakes of doing better are high. It is estimated that Bank financing reaches more than 11,000 cities and towns worldwide. Moreover, the implications of reform extend not only to urban services but also to much of the rest of the Bank's portfolio: to the social sectors, to nonurban infrastructure, and to national fiscal and income distribution policy. Improvements in local government performance are essential to protecting the urban environment and meeting the needs of poor populations for such services as clean water, sanitation, health, and education.

Focusing on the system of intergovernmental relations and the incentives local governments face is *timely* because change in this area is already under way. Of the seventy-five developing and transitional countries with populations over 5 million, all but twelve have initiated some form of transfer of political power to local units of government. However, the decentralization that is now occurring is not necessarily a carefully designed sequence of reforms aimed at improving public sector performance; rather, decentralization is a response to a complex set of pressures for change unique to the country in which it takes place. *Nevertheless, because decentralization has introduced a high degree of fluidity into the structure of intergovernmental relations, it presents borrower countries and external aid and lending institutions (including the Bank) with an opportunity to promote fundamental reforms that have not been possible in the past.* Other changes under way in many developing countries complement these reforms. The increased willingness to explore private sector involvement in the provision of public services, for example, permits more flexibility to adopt institutional arrangements that are conducive to good performance.

Directions for Reform

The constraints encountered in past institutional development efforts point to a conflict between the incentive structure confronting local government— what they are rewarded for—and the results that technical assistance sought to achieve by improving technical capacities and tools. Improved accounting systems sometimes fell into disuse or proved irrelevant because sound financial management at the local level was not rewarded. Improved technical systems for valuing real estate sometimes failed to generate the expected increases in property tax revenues because less politically sensitive sources of funds were available. Some of the improvements in the allocation of capital funding to local governments were not sustained and replicated because competing sources of capital funding were allocated on a less rigorous basis. Local service delivery appears to be a problem that cannot be addressed merely through the transfer of technical knowledge to local staff. Instead it is necessary to address the incentives implicit in the institutional arrangements for local service delivery—the rules governing the relationship between central government, local government, and local service consumers.

A number of considerations should go into the design of better institutional arrangements. Concern for allocative efficiency—that is, responsiveness to local preferences—suggests assignment of responsibility for specific public services to the level of government whose boundaries incorporate the affected beneficiaries—the principle of subsidiarity. It also follows that local governments taking on service responsibilities should be assigned a corresponding source of finance, preferably one that allows pricing to determine and manage demand effectively. Concern for technical efficiency related to the capacities of local governments, the optimal size of operations, and the potential role of the private sector in the delivery of services is another important consideration. An essential ingredient in improving the performance of organizations is the motivation of employees. It is increasingly recognized that the system of formal and informal rewards and sanctions that affect those involved in urban service delivery—not just their nominal powers and responsibilities—is an important determinant of performance. This approach directs attention to such issues as whether the mayor is appointed or elected, what determines the career trajectory of successful municipal managers, and the mechanisms by which interest groups, especially the users of urban services, can make their wishes known. *It is clear that reform in this area cannot be reduced to simple formulas. The complexity of individual country contexts and potential conflicts among the above considerations must be weighed in determining the direction, pace, and sequencing of a program for reform.* The experience of industrial countries, which might be presumed to provide models, is characterized by considerable variety and frequent experimentation and thus supports a flexible approach.

The evidence nonetheless suggests that three elements are crucial to the reform of the structure of urban service delivery: a clear division of functional responsibilities between levels of government, revenue sources corresponding to functional responsibilities, and clear accountability that encompasses both regulation by central government and incentives for responsiveness to local constituents.

Clear Responsibilities

Clarity in the division of functional responsibilities between levels of government is an essential condition of any reform in the structure of urban service delivery. *A clear linkage between a particular unit of government and a specific service is crucial if constituents are to hold that unit of government accountable for providing that service well.* Although open-ended central government involvement in nominally local responsibilities is often intended to compensate for local service failures, it undermines clear accountability for sound management of local service delivery. Clarity requires more than the de jure allocation of responsibilities that often bears little resemblance to actual practice. Making clear functional assignments credible requires, among other things, a system of managerial and financial discretion (and consequent accountability) that permits local governments to perform successfully the tasks that have been assigned to them or to "fail" openly if they manage them poorly. It may also require governments to legislate more geographic specificity into their municipal organic laws, to allow for differentiation among local governments according to their capacity to assume different functions.

Assigning responsibility to a level of government does not necessarily imply that the government should be the direct producer of the service in question. Involvement of the private sector can help to improve performance in the delivery of a variety of municipal services. Governments should actively seek out the opportunities for mobilizing private sector expertise and finance, while seeking to reduce unnecessary regulatory barriers to private sector involvement. In this regard, the recommendations of *World Development Report 1994* regarding enhanced private sector involvement in the delivery of infrastructure services are highly relevant and complementary to reforms in intergovernmental relations (World Bank 1994).

Revenue Reform

Reform in revenue assignments is needed if a clear division of functional responsibilities is to be credible and sustainable. The particular structure of local revenues—the mix of user charges, taxes, transfers, and loans—that is appropriate in a given context depends, first and foremost, on the functions that have been assigned to local government. Where the benefits of a service are largely confined to individual consumers, user charges are a desirable means of financing municipal services. Local taxes, in principle, are an appropriate means of financing services whose benefits, though not confined to individual consumers, nevertheless do not extend beyond the municipal boundaries. *Typically, local revenue sources are limited and heavily regulated by central government. Generally speaking, local governments need more financial autonomy to perform the responsibilities they have been assigned.*

Any attempt to reform the structure of urban service delivery, however, must also address the largest source of local revenue: intergovernmental transfers. Transfers can serve several important positive roles in the financing of municipal services, permitting central governments to induce local governments to undertake sectoral expenditures that are of national—rather than local—interest and to use local governments as agents of national income redistribution policies. But reform is required both to increase the effectiveness of transfers in achieving these sectoral and distributional objectives and to reduce the adverse side effects of badly targeted or badly administered transfers.

Perhaps the most important measure governments can take is to reduce the uncertainty and bargaining that now accompany intergovernmental financial flows. Governments also need to design transfer programs to finance adequately those activities that local governments undertake on behalf of the central government to meet national objectives—particularly if these include primary education and preventive health care—and to target them more effectively.

Reform is also needed in the arrangements municipal governments use to obtain access to financing for capital investment. *Improvements in allocation can be achieved by improving the targeting of grant programs, particularly where the preconditions for allocation by lending do not exist.*

But there is also a case for replacing grant financing with loan financing. Municipal credit institutions (MCIs) are an increasingly popular means of administering such programs. The performance of these organizations is mixed, however, and although legal and organizational measures can enhance their viability, experience suggests that what matters most is a government's commitment to the municipal credit institution's independence and its willingness to provide a supportive financial environment.

Balance of Central Regulation and Local Accountability

The extent to which a system of urban service delivery should rely on accountability upward to central government (through regulation) or downward to constituents is not an issue that lends itself to universal prescription. Balance is advisable.

Some degree of accountability to central government through a national regulatory framework is appropriate to any structure of urban service delivery. Central regulation is clearly needed where local government behavior can affect national policies—in areas ranging from macroeconomic stabilization to poverty and the environment. Central regulation is also appropriate where local governments are carrying out functions on behalf of central government. Systems of local accountability for purely local affairs are often desirable but take time to develop. In some cases, as a transitional measure, it may be necessary for central governments to exercise some oversight or regulatory control over local government affairs when local systems are weak. But where the impact of local government behavior is largely localized and regulation requires detailed knowledge of local conditions and priorities, central regulation is difficult to justify. In many developing countries, a relaxation of broad central regulation is called for, while more focused measures are needed to ensure local government performance in areas of national concern such as poverty alleviation and the environment.

The counterpart to central regulation is local accountability—the reliance on local participation to regulate the behavior of those responsible for managing service delivery. In Western countries especially, local elections are traditionally viewed as a key instrument for this purpose. However, even in countries with well-established electoral processes, supplementary measures are typically needed. The advent of local democracy, although increasingly common, is therefore no panacea. Moreover, the view that local elections always successfully ensure accountability does not stand up to scrutiny. The validity of elections after long periods of authoritarian rule appears particularly questionable. The reasons for this are not all well understood, but the absence of a tradition of community action, the lack of information, and poor communications appear to play an important role. There is some evidence that specific changes in election rules can influence the degree to which local elections function as referenda on local government performance. For example, scheduling elections off the national election cycle and allowing re-election or reasonably long terms for mayors seem to have promise. Finally, and probably of more significance in most developing countries, are alternative and supplementary means of increasing the effectiveness of local participation. Although there are no simple formulas, many local governments could take measures to ensure more regular consultation with constituents, develop stronger channels for monitoring user satisfaction with local services, and link career progression of civil servants more strongly to their responsiveness to constituents.

Synchronization and Interdependence of Reform Measures

Although there are different ways to organize the delivery of urban services, the various pieces of the intergovernmental relationship should fit together coherently. This has become increasingly evident in a number of countries now undergoing structural changes. In many cases, central governments have been prompted to make political concessions, steps that can typically be taken quickly. What is slow and difficult is the working through of new regulatory relationships between central government and local government, the conversion of what had been annual budgetary transfers within a central government into intergovernmental transfers that are transparent and predictable, and the development of local political systems with broad accountability and responsiveness. *Many of the problems associated with the current wave of decentralization arise from the failure to match the pace of political change to the pace of regulatory and other organizational reforms described above.*

Implications for the World Bank

This report supports strengthening the approach to building institutions for urban service delivery that is already evident in some Bank work—*that is, a shift away from placing a primary emphasis on the internal administration of local government and toward an understanding of urban service delivery as a problem that involves the structure of the entire public sector, particularly the relationship between central and local government.* The Bank should operationalize this viewpoint more broadly and effectively. This effort will involve change in both how and by whom this issue is handled.

Country Strategies

The multisectoral dimension of urban service delivery suggests the need for the government and the Bank to *develop country-specific strategies for promoting the reform of intergovernmental relations and local institutional arrangements.* This approach would help to ensure consistency both in the Bank's dialog with national government on macroeconomic and distributional issues and in the range of sectors in which the Bank is active. It would also ensure that adequate attention is given to the range of systemic problems that affect the performance of a number of sectors in a cost-effective fashion.

These country strategies should attempt to define a limited number of key issues viewed as critical to performance in local service delivery, to the productivity and sustainability of projects, and to broader economywide development goals such as poverty alleviation and private sector development. Identification of these issues should be based on an analysis of the present structure of the public sector, with particular attention to the institutional framework and incentives embodied therein. These issues should become part of the regular dialog between the Bank and the government at the national level. *Progress on the systemwide institutional reform agenda should be a regular part of discussions of country strategy, portfolio performance review, and economic and sector work; it should also be weighed as a factor in determining the sectoral composition and size of the lending program.*

Lending

Reform in those areas identified as critical to local service delivery should become a key criterion against which investment projects are judged. A variety of lending instruments can be vehicles for pursuing the reform agenda. Achieving the institutional changes that are needed in many countries will usually require sustained efforts over a sequence of individual investment operations, with strong policy content and follow-through in the policy dialog. Innovative financial intermediation projects for municipal investments that have been used to achieve broad-based reform of intergovernmental relationships (typically financial transfers) are an example of an approach to investment lending that can support systemwide reforms. Sectoral adjustment lending, most likely coupled with technical assistance, is also a promising option.

Consistent with this approach, attention to systemwide reform issues must be spread more evenly over the project cycle, if investment lending is to serve as a vehicle to promote fundamental change. The types of issues that are involved can rarely be addressed in the relatively short period of project preparation. The Bank should take greater advantage of opportunities to promote institutional reform through sector work prior to appraisal and through supervision and consideration of further operations. Preproject sector work provides the opportunity for the Bank and governments to reach an understanding on reform outside the time-bound environment of loan negotiations.

Research, Policy, and Sector Work

The Bank also needs to enhance substantially its ability to deal with subnational institutional issues by deepening its understanding of the determinants of public sector performance. As this book demonstrates, the operational implications of more knowledge in this area are substantial. There are three main areas where further research is urgently needed. First, how does devolution of responsibility to lower levels of government affect key variables that we know are related to the effectiveness of local services: among others, unit cost of services, cost recovery, spending for maintenance as opposed to new investments, involvement of the private sector, and the capacity to mobilize private sector financing for infrastructure investments. A second, related question is how intergovernmental financing arrangements affect local government performance. It is well recognized that the financing arrangements accompanying any restructuring of responsibilities for service delivery are crucial. However, we need answers to more specific operational questions. For example, how well do "rules-based" systems function in practice in encouraging sound local financial management? To what extent are earmarking and other forms of conditionality effective in encouraging local expenditures on services of national interest? How does the structure of intergovernmental transfers affect macroeconomic performance in decentralizing systems? Finally, the Bank needs to assess better the interaction between systems of institutional incentives and capacity strengthening within institutions. We need to learn more about how to design technical assistance that reinforces good institutional incentive systems and about the role technical assistance can play in a transition to better institutional arrangements.

An important vehicle in the learning process will be structured learning from operational work. Bank-supported projects offer a broad range of opportunities to gather evidence systematically on how different institutional arrangements affect local service performance in specific country contexts. This learning aspect of operational work can be enhanced by directing more specific attention to these issues in project design and then by following through in supervision. Building a systematic learning process more directly into the design and implementation of projects would not only help to establish a better knowledge base for the Bank's future work but also play an essential role in building borrower commitment to alternative institutional arrangements.

Introduction

THE developing world is being transformed from a world of rural villages into a world of cities and towns. In 1960 less than 22 percent of the population of low- and middle-income countries was urban. By 1990 that proportion had increased by roughly half, to 34 percent. The urbanization of the developing world is a global phenomenon, extending to every region in which the World Bank operates. All the major regions of the world have experienced dramatic increases in urbanization in the last quarter century (figure 1.1), and it is projected that by the year 2020, more than half of the population of developing countries will be urban. In those countries in 1990, there were twenty-four cities with at least 5 million people; in 2020, there will likely be more than sixty (United Nations 1993).

National economies are also increasingly urban. Although figures on the geographic origin of gross domestic product (GDP) are difficult to obtain, sectoral data indicate the importance of cities in national economies. In 1990 more than 80 percent of the GDP of the low- and middle-income countries was produced in the nonagricultural sectors—largely in manufacturing and services. And data on the sectoral composition of economic *growth* suggest that the urban sector is a principal engine of development. Growth rates in manufacturing and services consistently exceeded those in agriculture in virtually all regions of the world during the past decade (table 1.1). Even in regions undergoing severe adjustment during the 1980s, growth rates in manufacturing and services far exceeded those in agriculture.

Figure 1.1   Trends in World Urbanization: Percentage of Population Living in Cities by Developing Region, 1960, 1990, and 2020

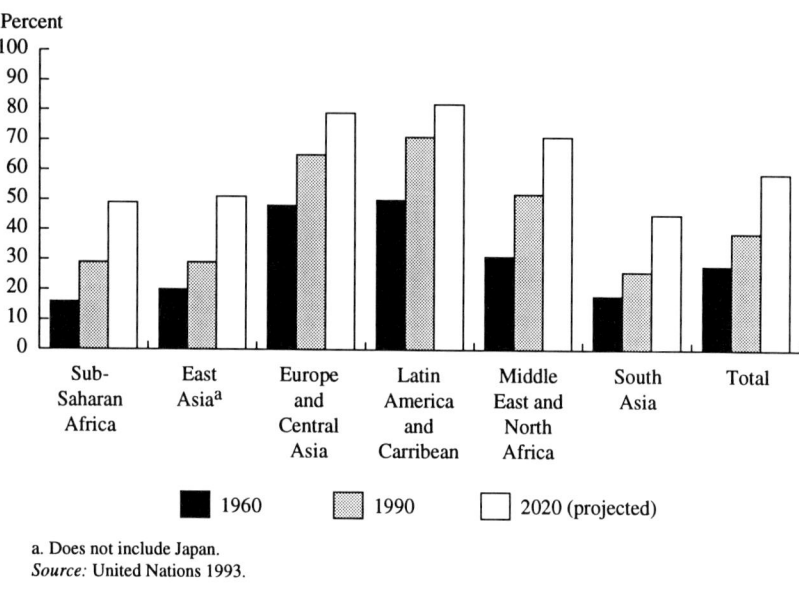

a. Does not include Japan.
Source: United Nations 1993.

The demographic growth of cities and their contribution to national economies suggest that cities work. Urban population growth is fueled by the prospects for jobs and higher incomes. The available evidence suggests that these expectations have largely been met. The personal income of rural-to-urban migrants typically rises. Higher incomes in cities, in turn, reflect the greater productivity of labor in cities: studies of labor productivity suggest that urban-rural wage differentials largely reflect spatial variations in labor productivity.

Yet cities do not deliver on the promise of a better quality of life to the extent they could. Despite the relatively high incomes of urban populations, the quality of services in major cities is poor. At least 170 million people in urban areas lack a source of potable water near their homes, and in many cases, the water that is supplied to those who have access is polluted. Nearly 350 million people in urban areas lack access to basic sanitation—a figure that is believed to have increased in absolute terms over the past decade. (These data are from the World Health Organization, as cited in World Bank 1992.) In many large cities in developing countries, less than 70 percent of municipal solid wastes are collected and only 50 percent of households are served (Bartone, Bernstein, and Wright 1990). In Mexico City the average commute to work is between 2.5 and 3.5 hours (Legorreta and Flores 1989). Although data on the coverage of education and health services in urban areas are not available, the aggregate statistics for developing countries are disturbing: in half of low-income countries, fewer than half of school-age children are enrolled in primary schools (World Bank 1990).

These service failures have wider economic and distributional implications. Improving urban service delivery is essential to any strategy to protect the urban environment. Recent work on the infrastructure sectors notes that a lack of access to, or the unreliability of, infrastructure services can have adverse effects on growth, forcing firms to seek more expensive alternatives, which may in turn have unfavorable impacts on profits and levels of production and consequently on investment and job growth (Kessides 1993b). A 1988 study of manufacturing establishments in Nigeria found that the costs of private substitutes for public infrastructure services (generators, boreholes, vehicles for personnel and freight transport, and radio communications equipment) constituted 25 percent of the total machinery and equipment costs of small firms and 10 percent of large firms (Lee and Anas 1992).

Service failures also have distributional implications. The economic benefits of urbanization have not been uniformly distributed. As countries have urbanized, poverty has urbanized as well. It is now roughly estimated that about 25 percent of urban populations are poor, which represents about 400 million people. Failures in urban service delivery disproportion-

Table 1.1   Average Annual Growth of GDP, by Developing Region and Sector, 1980–90

(percent)

Region	Agriculture	Manufacturing	Services
Sub-Saharan Africa	2.1	3.1	2.5
East Asia	4.8	12.4	8.0
South Asia	3.0	6.8	6.3
Europe	1.0	—	2.7
Middle East and North Africa	4.3	3.4	1.9
Latin America	1.0	1.7	1.7

— Not available.
Source: World Bank 1992b.

ately affect the poor. As a result, many poor households must resort to alternatives that often imply not only lower quality but higher costs. In the absence of piped water supply systems, for example, households are forced to purchase water from vendors, at several multiples of the costs of piped water systems.

The Management Problem

Failures in the coverage and quality of services reflect, in part, aggregate resource constraints. The ability of an economy to provide convenient, reliable urban services is constrained by the demands of other fundamental needs—food, clothing, basic shelter, and security—in extremely poor countries. *But the available evidence suggests that the constraint on improved service delivery is not merely one of resources. The level of resources already devoted to urban service delivery is substantial.* There is evidence, for example, that in the absence of conventional service delivery systems, households commonly resort to more expensive alternative sources. In Jakarta, Indonesia, 800,000 households have installed septic tanks, at a cost equal to three times the amount that would have been required to provide connections to condominial piped sewerage systems. Moreover, there is evidence that governments, particularly central governments, already spend a significant amount on urban services. Although statistics on the sectoral and geographic pattern of government expenditure are scarce (particularly in developing countries), estimates of the annual level of central government expenditure on urban services in the developing and transition economies range from $100 billion to $200 billion, approximately 2.5 percent to 5.0 percent of GDP.[1] *The deficiencies in urban services in the cities of developing countries are therefore a reflection not merely of absolute resource constraints but also of other constraints, particularly the institutional arrangements of urban service delivery.*

Describing the institutional arrangements of urban service delivery is an ambitious task. The traditional focus of institutional development was the organization. The objective was to improve the organization's ability to make effective use of available resources, a task that would be accomplished through the application of good technique (civil service reform, organizational planning, financial analysis).

More recently, frustration with this approach has prompted a change in strategy toward institutional analysis, with a shift in focus away from the organization and toward the incentive structure, that is, the various rewards and penalties confronting the individuals involved in the delivery of urban services.[2] In part, this represents a shift in how the internal operations of an

organization are addressed: a change in focus from administrative procedures to the factors motivating individuals within the organization. But it
also directs attention to the role played by individuals *outside* the organization: the consumer interest groups, unions, and central government regu-
lators whose behavior also influences the performance of service delivery
systems. While not denying the importance of administrative procedures,
this view would argue that procedural reforms are only effective if the
incentive structure is supportive; that what matters in the first instance, for
example, is not the accounting system, but the motivation of the staff to
use it (Ostrom, Schroeder, and Wynne 1992).

This perspective suggests that difficulties in service delivery are in
part due to systemwide problems rather than to problems within organizations alone. One of the major issues some have identified is heavy centralization of the public sector. Critics of the often centralized structure of
government in developing countries argue that such structures are inherently incapable of responsive administration. Because the concerns of central government[3] become increasingly predominant as the locus of
decisionmaking moves away from beneficiaries, because the costs of influence become increasingly high as decisions are centralized, and because the quality of information about local conditions becomes increasingly
distorted as it moves from field officers to central administration, centralized political and administrative systems have relatively weak incentives
to respond to local needs. Rondinelli, for example, argues that "rarely do
incentives exist for central government ministries to perceive citizens as
their clientele" (Rondinelli 1990).

This view is echoed in the Bank's work. Winkler's study of decentralization in education, for example, notes that arguments for decentralization
typically cite the costs of decisionmaking in a system where "even the
most minor local education matters must be decided by a geographically
and culturally distant bureaucracy in the capital city and where education
ministries frequently apply national standards for curriculum, construction, teacher quality, etc., thereby preventing cost savings through adjustments of educational inputs to local or regional price differences" (Winkler
1991). Heggie's work on the transport sector similarly argues that "it is
clear at the national level that it is difficult to achieve accountability because of the heterogeneity of users and their remoteness from the center of
government" (Heggie 1991). Decentralization is often cited as the solution
to these problems. (Although the generic term "decentralization" refers to
a variety of organizational reforms, here it refers only to the transfer of
decisionmaking power from central governments to subnational political
entities; see box 1.1.)

**BOX 1.1 A TYPOLOGY
OF DECENTRALIZATION**

Rondinelli's classic typology identifies four categories of decentralization. All represent transfers of power from central government administration. The typology distinguishes types of decentralization on the basis of the organization to which power is transferred.

Deconcentration is defined as a transfer of power to local administrative offices of the central government; *delegation* is the transfer of power to parastatals; *devolution* is the transfer of power to subnational political entities; *privatization* is the transfer of power (and responsibility) to private entities.

Source: Rondinelli 1990.

As later chapters of this book will show, centralization versus decentralization is just one of a range of aspects of the institutional arrangements governing local service delivery that can have an important impact on performance. Decentralization is of particular significance because it is already happening on the ground and demonstrates the timeliness of pursuing systemwide institutional reform. Political decentralization is, in fact, a widespread phenomenon. Of the seventy-five developing and transitional countries with populations of more than 5 million (as defined in World Bank 1993b), all but twelve have initiated some form of transfer of political power to local units of government. The form and extent of decentralization vary. In parts of Africa, national governments are creating local political entities in territories that were formerly solely under the administration of central government. In Eastern Europe, what were formerly local administrative units of the central government have been transformed into separate political entities, with leadership chosen by local election rather than by appointment through the party structure. In Latin America, similarly, decentralization has meant a shift from centrally appointed mayors to mayors chosen by election. (In some Latin American and African countries, the most significant aspect of decentralization is the central government's tolerance of local victories by opposition parties.) In some countries, particularly in Latin America, political decentralization has been accompanied by increases in revenue sharing or by nominal changes in the legal definition of local functional responsibilities.

But the immediate motivations for decentralization, as it is observed in practice, appear to be only tangentially related to administrative reform. The decentralization that is now occurring is not typically a carefully designed sequence of reforms aimed at improving public sector performance.

Rather it is a response to a complex set of pressures for change as varied as the country contexts in which it takes place.

Whatever the motivating forces behind recent political decentralization, in practice it has not necessarily brought about improvements in service delivery. Unfortunate administrative consequences of decentralization are evident in a variety of contexts:

■ In Hungary, the concession of local political autonomy preceded the separation of local budgets from the central government budgeting system (Bird and Wallich 1992). As a result, local governments lack a financially sustainable revenue base (raising the prospect that the social safety net, for which local governments bear major responsibility, will run out of funds in the near future).

■ In Brazil, where decentralization was reportedly motivated by the political repudiation of two decades of military rule, decentralization took the form of a substantial increase in revenue sharing and in the taxing powers of local government (Shah 1991). It was not, however, accompanied by a corresponding delineation of local expenditure responsibilities. Thus, although local governments have more money to spend, they are no more accountable for the quality of their services than they were before the reforms.

■ In Ghana, political decentralization has not, so far, been accompanied by a commensurate decentralization of authority: the creation of locally elected legislative bodies has not been accompanied by a transfer of significant decisionmaking authority to local government. The Ghanaian government continues to appoint the municipal executive and the heads of municipal departments and effectively controls local spending decisions.

Relevance to the World Bank

Despite these shortcomings, the important changes in the structure of government responsibilities now under way—which are commonly referred to as decentralization—still present an opportunity to promote administrative reform because they have introduced a high degree of fluidity in the structure of the public sector. Experience shows that these structural issues have an important impact on the performance of local governments. Moreover, appropriate changes in intergovernmental relationships are complementary to other reform initiatives such as increased private sector involvement, where appropriate, to improve the delivery of public infrastructure services. The opportunity for change is one that the World Bank and the external aid and lending community, but more important the countries themselves, should grasp.

The potential impacts of such reforms may extend beyond sectors that the World Bank has traditionally defined as urban. Changes in the allocation of power between levels of government have implications for national efforts to reduce poverty and to manage the macroeconomy (particularly to the extent to which they reduce central control over the instruments of fiscal policy, according to Prud'homme 1994). Stronger local government performance also affects the delivery of social services—primary education and health—as well as nonurban infrastructure. Intergovernmental relations are in fact already the subject of Bank sector work in education, transport, and health.

There is no road map here. The world is witnessing more than 200 ongoing experiments with decentralization. Of the countries that have embarked on programs of decentralization, none yet has a record of experience that would permit an ex post evaluation. The industrial economies, which might be assumed to offer models, have themselves adopted different approaches to the organization of their subnational governments, and several are in a constant state of experimentation. The objective of this book is therefore modest: to document the Bank's past approach to the development of (urban) local governments, to derive lessons from that experience, and to propose an approach (derived from both theory and experience) that might be used in the future.

CHAPTER TWO

A Review of Experience

THE World Bank has, since its inception, supported efforts to improve public service delivery. The establishment of an urban lending program in the early 1970s gave particular focus to work on municipal institutions. Around that time, a number of other members of the external aid and lending community became more involved in urban issues as well. Experience in the sector over the past twenty years provides a number of lessons about what works well and what does not and has helped to refine considerably our sense of what is needed to improve the performance of municipal institutions in delivering urban services. This survey focuses on experience with the municipal development efforts embodied in urban lending.

The First Decade

Beginning in 1972, urban lending focused primarily on urban *housing*; specifically, the problem of supplying affordable housing to low-income populations. The intent of initial urban lending was to demonstrate the feasibility of low-cost solutions to the housing problems of rapidly growing cities. In pursuing this agenda, the Bank relied largely on demonstration projects: sites and services and upgrading projects aimed at demonstrating the feasibility of low-cost approaches to the provision of residential infrastructure. Many other external aid and lending institutions followed a similar approach in this period.

The principal interlocutors for these projects were usually central government housing or public works ministries. Projects often required the creation of executing agencies capable of coordinating investments across sectors in a single site. This problem was typically resolved by the creation of special project units, separate from the existing institutional structure. These were often organizational branches of a national (or in the large federal countries, state) government (see table 2.1).

These projects were generally successful in meeting their physical investment targets. In fact, internal Bank reviews have found that the urban sector consistently ranked among the highest-performing sectors (with 83 percent of projects evaluated as successful). However, early on, difficulties were encountered in ensuring that the project units continued to carry out their planning and coordination role after project completion. In addition, as projects neared completion, arrangements for operations and maintenance did not always work out as planned. Often, municipal governments lacked the technical and financial capacity to assume responsibility for the operation and maintenance of new facilities.

These "handover" problems led fairly rapidly to a shift in project design. Projects increasingly included components aimed at improving the

Table 2.1   Executing Agencies in World Bank–financed Urban Development Projects

Country and city	Executing agency	Description
Côte d'Ivoire	SETU	Government land development agency
Kenya: Nairobi	HDD	Special unit within local government
Senegal: sites and services	DPA	Special unit under government housing agency
India: Calcutta	CMDA	Metro development agency, reporting to state government
Indonesia	KIP unit	DKI: government of the capital district (headed by government appointee)
Brazil: sites and services	COHAB	State housing companies
Mexico: Lázaro	FIDELAC	Government special commission
Colombia	SIP	Government popular housing institute
Morocco	Ministry of Housing	Government housing ministry

performance of municipal governments so that they could take on the roles they were expected to play. These efforts were focused on internal municipal administration—where the problems were most immediately apparent. Approximately two-thirds of the identifiable targets of Bank-supported municipal development efforts during this period were aimed at local taxation, accounting, or capital budgeting. A number of other members of the external aid and lending community, particularly the United Kingdom and the United States, took a similar approach.

The most common single object of Bank-assisted municipal development efforts during this period was the property tax. In the first decade of its urban lending operations, the Bank financed thirty projects with components aimed at increasing property tax revenues. In helping governments improve local property tax yields, the Bank relied on varying combinations of loan conditionality and technical assistance. Loan conditionality under the first (Kenya) Nairobi Site and Service Project, for example, engaged the government, first, to undertake a study of municipal finance in Kenya and, second, to take such actions as would be required to permit the Nairobi local authority (NCC) to maintain a reasonable level of recurrent and development expenditure, a condition that was ultimately interpreted as requiring a general increase in property valuations. Under the first Calcutta Urban Development Project, the government of West Bengal undertook (as a loan condition) to "formulate a plan for improving the financial performance of municipalities within the Calcutta metropolitan district." The plan, which recommended the creation of a central property valuation board for the Calcutta metropolitan area, was the basis for loan conditionality in the subsequent second Calcutta project, which required the revaluation of properties in the metropolitan region. In Indonesia, similarly, the sequence of property tax interventions began with a study of the property tax system (financed under a preceding engineering credit). Loan conditionality under the first urban project then required the government to implement the study's major recommendation—to change the basis of assessment—and to increase actual revenues in the project city at a rate of 15 percent annually in real terms during the disbursement period. Subsequent projects in other regions also focused on minimum levels of annual increase in property tax revenue. The Sixth Indonesia Urban Development Project—an urban sector loan—directly financed a revaluation by private consultants of properties in Jakarta. Cadastral surveys were also financed under the Brazil medium-size cities project and in a series of urban and municipal development projects in the Philippines.

Municipal accounting practices were also commonly addressed in municipal development efforts supported by the external aid and lending

Table 2.2   Technical Assistance for Accounting

Project	Assistance
Kenya (secondary towns)	Technical assistance for improving accounting procedures
Turkey (Cukurova)	Technical assistance for design and implementation of new accounting procedures
Indonesia (Urban III)	Introduction of program budgeting in Surabaya
India (Madras)	Technical assistance for design and implementation of new accounting procedures
Colombia (Urban I)	Technical assistance for study of municipal information system
Brazil (Paraná, market towns)	Institutional development program (package of technical assistance for financial and accounting practices)

community. Technical assistance to promote better accounting and budgeting procedures was included in many Bank-supported municipal development projects (see table 2.2).

The results of the work on tax administration and accounting included some successes but often met with important limitations. Some very important lessons were learned in the process. The agencies we assisted often did not have full autonomy to act on the technical recommendations they received. Sometimes the problem was one of administrative authority. Probably more often, the political costs of raising taxes or improving transparency in accounting relative to softer options such as discretionary central government transfers were a more serious impediment than had been realized. Increasingly, it was recognized that the decisionmakers typically faced little reward and many penalties for taking the actions envisaged as part of improving municipal financial capacity. As Israel, among others, has noted, "commitment" is not a random or independent factor (Israel 1987). Project participants can be expected to be committed to actions that they perceive to be in their interest and to remain uncommitted to those that are not.

With the benefit of hindsight and a heightened understanding of the role of local governments in an era of decentralization, another more fundamental lesson can be drawn from this experience. How well technical assistance succeeded in improving municipal revenues may not have been the most significant measure of success for municipal development efforts.

If, as this review argues, improving the performance of municipal services should be the objective of municipal development, whether or not municipalities were able to improve their modest resource mobilization and budgeting capacity was only of secondary importance. Municipalities in many developing countries played only a modest role in municipal service delivery. Decisions concerning major urban capital works were made by national sector ministries, and even the level of municipal operating revenue depended more on success in negotiating intergovernmental transfers than on local tax effort. Local resource mobilization was important, but only as part of a much larger and more complex institutional environment—one in which ambiguities in the assignment of functional responsibilities, distortionary transfers, and the absence of systems of local accountability were major constraints on sound urban service delivery.

The Second Decade

Bank work in the 1980s exhibited a shift consistent with these lessons. The conclusion of the first decade of urban lending was marked by a dramatic increase in studies of urban institutions (see figure 2.1). In the first nine years of urban lending (1972–80), the Bank produced only seven urban sector studies that addressed local institutional issues. During the following four years, it produced twenty-eight.

Figure 2.1 Studies of Local Institutions, 1973–92

Number of studies

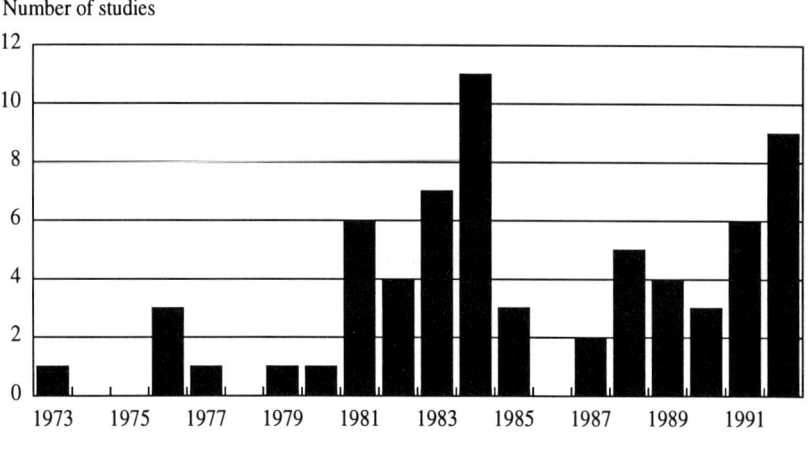

The content of sector work focused increasingly on structural issues. Intergovernmental fiscal relations were addressed in several sector studies. A study of local government and decentralization in Mexico noted, for example, that the distribution of transfers between jurisdictions needed review. It found that the current system caused considerable distortions at the municipal level, which were unacceptable on both efficiency and equity grounds. Recognition of the link between transfers and local tax effort was reflected in a study in Brazil, which found that the overall design of municipal funding and in particular the design of transfers did not provide incentives to municipalities to maximize their own revenue. A review of local government finance in Pakistan addressed the assignment of functional responsibilities, noting that in large urban areas, the existence of state-owned development authorities gave rise to duplication and overlap in service provision. This duplication created inefficiencies in the allocation and use of public resources. It also created a framework that reduces incentives for local government to raise further resources and encourages a shifting of responsibility for incremental service expenditure onto higher tiers of government. A study of Kenya addressed the issue of central regulation of local government, noting that excessive intervention often begets a vicious cycle. The more government intervenes, the more irresponsible councils become; the more irresponsible councils become, the more government intervenes.

This broader perspective was also reflected in the subsequent lending program. The number of urban projects with municipal development components increased dramatically beginning in 1983 (see figure 2.2). Between 1972 and 1982, an average of three projects a year with municipal development components were approved. Between 1983 and 1992, the average increased to eight. The institutional focus of these projects also broadened. Although municipal development projects continued to finance technical assistance for the internal management of municipal government (taxation, accounting, and capital budgeting), there was increased attention to the institutional environment in which local government operates. This was reflected in the loan conditionality and technical assistance. The Sri Lanka Municipal Management Project, for example, financed technical assistance for rationalizing the grants system, monitoring the newly introduced incentives system for the allocation of funds on the basis of performance, and studying the feasibility of a municipal loan fund. In connection with the Indonesia Urban Sector Loan, similarly, the government agreed to reforms in the structure of local access to credit and in the system of intergovernmental grants.

Figure 2.2   Trends in Municipal Development Projects, 1972–92

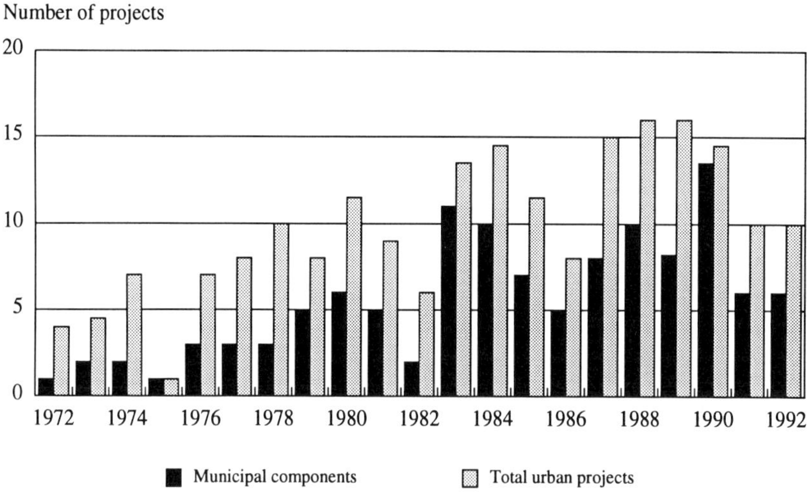

Number of projects

Legend: ■ Municipal components   ▨ Total urban projects

   Most frequently, the means by which the Bank became involved, on a national scale, in the structure of urban service delivery was through municipal infrastructure fund projects—an approach also adopted by some other members of the external aid and lending community. Bank-supported projects in particular attempted to reform the mechanisms for financing local capital investment on a countrywide basis and thus to address intergovernmental institutional issues. In these projects, the Bank, in effect, built on its role as a source of external capital financing to promote reform in the procedures used to allocate capital financing domestically and to induce broader reforms in the performance of local government.

   From 1980 to 1992, twenty-five municipal infrastructure fund operations were approved by the Bank. Table 2.3 provides details on the measures supported under a sample of these projects. The primary focus of these projects was on the criteria used to allocate capital financing among local governments. Bank-assisted projects typically attempted to introduce systematic economic and financial criteria into what was perceived as an excessively arbitrary system of funding distribution. The first Jordan Cities and Villages Development Project (in 1980), for example, was accompanied by the adoption of a policy statement establishing criteria by which

Table 2.3   Measures Supported in Municipal Credit Projects

Project	*Measures*
Jordan: CVDB (1980, 1985)	Support transformation of development fund into bank, reform in project selection criteria
Morocco: FEC (1983)	Reform eligibility criteria for project selection, emphasize cost recovery
Calcutta (1983)	Create fund to lend to small-scale, locally initiated public works
Brazil: Paraná (1983, 1989)	Introduce lending component into state capital grant program (first project); reform eligibility criteria (second project)
Philippines: MP (1984, 1989, 1992)	Establish fund to lend to locally initiated projects; impose financial, institutional conditionality
Mexico: FORTAMUN (1986)	Establish fund to lend to locally initiated projects, at near-market rates, explicit selection criteria
Indonesia sector loan	"Policy agreement" and study to create municipal credit institution
Turkey: Cukurova (1987)	Study to transform government public works agency into infrastructure bank
Nigeria: MDF	Using merchant banks as intermediaries, establish fund to finance locally initiated projects on self-selection basis
Argentina (1988)	Create funds in five provinces to impose institutional, financial conditionality
India: Tamil Nadu (1988)	Create fund to lend to locally initiated projects; impose institutional, financial criteria
Zimbabwe (1989)	Reform eligibility criteria in existing fund
Côte d'Ivoire	Establish fund to lend to locally initiated projects
Ecuador	Create fund within existing development bank; impose financial, institutional eligibility; raise interest rate
Colombia: FINDETER	Expand existing government, rediscounting window for locally initiated projects (financial risk held by private banks)

municipal eligibility would be determined. The focus of the first Morocco project, similarly, was to assist FEC (the intermediary) in setting up coherent operating procedures, particularly with respect to project financing, where the modalities of interventions, from receipt of financing requests to project approvals and supervision, would be formalized.

Projects also sought to change the terms on which governments provided funds for local capital works, encouraging a shift from grants to loans—both to reinforce the technocratic basis for distribution and to provide a future source of funding through the relending of debt service. The first Morocco project, for example, proposed an increase in FEC's lending rate and required a subsequent annual review of the lending rates to ensure a positive spread. Similarly, the first Paraná (Brazil) project introduced a loan element into what had formerly been a program of capital grants.

Projects have also sought to induce broader reforms in the management of recipient municipalities. Under the Third Calcutta Municipal Development Project, for example, a grant formula was introduced that explicitly rewarded improvement in property tax collection rates. Projects in Paraná (Brazil), and later in Argentina and Ecuador, required municipalities to present financial action plans (demonstrating either their creditworthiness or the specific actions to be taken to render themselves creditworthy) as conditions of eligibility. Projects also promoted local capital investment planning by requiring the production of a local capital investment plan as a condition of eligibility.

The institutional impact of these projects is, as yet, unclear, because these projects are relatively new. However, a few interesting patterns have emerged. It has been difficult to achieve both strong debt service recovery and adherence to project selection criteria, but in several cases one of these objectives was met. The Philippines and Paraná (Brazil) projects met both requirements but started in a narrow segment of the market. Follow-on projects in both countries were able either to broaden coverage or to strengthen local performance conditions. Competing sources of funds often undermined the effectiveness of the changes in the capital allocation rules supported in Bank-assisted projects. Experience also suggests that changing capital allocation rules alone without addressing recurrent intergovernmental transfers is not sufficient to change the behavior of local government.

More recent projects have sought to build on these lessons and represent moves in a promising direction. Three recent Bank-assisted projects, for example, focus on reform in both recurrent and capital intergovernmental transfers. Their focus is on systemwide changes in intergovernmental transfers rather than on project-related funding. The 1990 Ecuador Municipal Development Project supports a government initiative to replace a deficit-based intergovernmental transfer system with one based on a clearly defined distribution formula. The 1992 Morocco Municipal Finance Project supports the replacement of ad hoc transfers with a formula-based system and extends reform to systematic improvements in the allocation of capital finance. In Argentina, transfers to local governments are distributed by the provinces, so reform was sought at the provincial level. Only provinces willing to adopt acceptable formula-derived transfer systems were permitted to participate in the Municipal Development Project (1988). Moreover, action on these issues has been timed carefully. In the case of Argentina, satisfactory changes in provincial-to-municipal transfers were required before a province would be declared eligible for financing. In the case of Ecuador, changes in the national intergovernmental transfers system were made during project preparation.

Overall, the experience of past lending for municipal development suggests that the initial focus on the internal administration of municipal governments was important, but not sufficient. It is clear that problems in local tax administration and accounting did exist. But it is also clear that the scope of our assistance and policy dialog should not be confined to internal administration. The experience of urban lending suggests that broader problems in the structure of intergovernmental relations and incentives have an important impact on the performance of urban services, a key developmental objective. More narrowly, these issues have a bearing on the productivity and sustainability of the investments that the Bank and other members of the external aid and lending community support. Some of the more promising recent projects suggest that, indeed, these structural issues can be addressed in lending operations; to achieve the desired results, they should be a central feature of project design and overall policy dialog.

A Framework for Analysis

THE fact that interventions in internal administration alone have limited impacts on service performance has implications for the way in which this subject should be approached. It is now clear that municipal government, as an organization, does not encapsulate the problem with which we should ultimately be concerned, that is, the performance of urban services. The constraints on urban services do not lie only in factors that are under the ostensible control of local government. As noted earlier, in many countries, municipal governments have only a tangential role in municipal service delivery. Moreover, the performance of local government is influenced by central government regulatory and financial controls. Urban service delivery therefore appears to be a problem that cannot be addressed by taking the organizational context as given and attempting to change the behavior of one organization—municipal government—within it. Instead, it appears to be a problem of the public sector as a whole, and one that has to be addressed by looking at all the factors that influence the performance of specific urban services.

Although there are shortfalls in urban services that have serious economic and social consequences, there is no ipso facto case for giving urban service expenditure precedence over other types of public sector expenditure or over private consumption. In a world of scarce resources, urban services have to compete with alternative uses of funds. Thus, there is a case for increasing the *efficiency* of urban service delivery. This includes allocative efficiency—in other words, providing the level and mix of services

that reflect the preferences of consumers—and technical efficiency—
that is, producing the maximum output per unit of input.[1] The objective is
therefore to achieve not necessarily more output, but rather a level and mix
of outputs that reflect consumer preferences, produced at the lowest unit
costs permitted by technology and management practice.

These are not, however, the sole objectives of urban service reform.
Although there is a conceptual argument for focusing on efficiency in
local service provision, in practice these services cannot be separated from
other objectives of the public sector, particularly poverty alleviation and
macroeconomic stability.[2] Box 3.1 illustrates some of these linkages for
the case of Peru. Decisions on the level and financing of municipal services have important distributional implications: expenditures on education and health, for example, are often the most significant forms of transfers
to the poor in developing countries. Moreover, to the extent that central
governments effectively concede control over fiscal policy to local governments, certain financing arrangements can have adverse implications
for the pursuit of national policy objectives regarding trade, macroeconomic
stabilization, and the environment, among others. The objective of municipal service reform is therefore complex. Although efficiency (in both the
allocational and technical senses) may be paramount, implications for poverty and fiscal stability are also important.

Defining the Instruments

What are the means by which performance is improved? Despite the volu-
minous literature on this subject (from the fields of public administration,
public finance, and more recently, institutional economics), there is no
universal prescription. As Israel (1987) has noted, what must be changed is
the behavior of people in organizations, a phenomenon that defies simple
diagnosis and treatment. Several academic traditions, nevertheless, contribute the elements of a conceptual approach.

The *benefit jurisdiction model*—a product of the public finance field—
provides a useful starting point. In the classic text, efficiency in resource
allocation is recognized as one of the principal roles of the public sector
(Musgrave and Musgrave 1984). Where markets fail to allocate resources
efficiently, the public sector is required to do so. This does not imply that
the *central* government bears exclusive responsibility for resource allocation, however. Noting that the benefits of some services are confined to
local jurisdictions, and that tastes and preferences for such public services
vary among populations, it is argued that welfare gains can be achieved by
assigning decisionmaking control over these services to corresponding

BOX 3.1 MUNICIPAL MANAGEMENT
AND POVERTY: THE CASE OF PERU

The government of Peru has been intensively debating approaches to strengthening the management of municipal services. Access to, and the quality of, municipal-level services have been deteriorating, constraining productivity and the government's efforts to reduce poverty and improve urban environmental conditions. Well-functioning municipalities are necessary for sustainable solutions to these deteriorating conditions, but constraints imposed by central-local fiscal relationships, difficulties in financing and cost recovery, and administrative capacities limit the effectiveness of municipalities in Peru. As is so often the case, the impact is borne disproportionately by the poor.

Fortunately, there are unusual strengths and opportunities in the Peruvian situation, especially the strong community-based operations and the history of collaborative working relationships between community-based organizations (CBOs), nongovernmental organizations (NGOs), municipalities, and central agencies. In Peru, the lack of service delivery by local government has resulted in a variety of alternative local-level community-based services initiated by diverse local CBO and NGO groups. In the process of initiating such services, these groups have gained wide experience with the complex planning specificities and needs at the local level and expertise that can contribute to capacity building at the municipal level.

Given the context in which municipalities function, many of them are unable to deliver adequate and reliable services, frustrating the poor who consume those basic urban services and are willing to pay a high price for them. In contrast, collaborative CBO/NGO service delivery programs in general enjoy reasonable levels of credibility and relatively high repayment rates. This is understandable. When service users participate in the process of making decisions about service priorities, standards, and methods of delivery, they must confront the issue of cost. Further, when management is closer to service users, clearer responsibility, authority, and accountability may be anticipated. Sacrifices in technical efficiency and economies of scale are often compensated by user responsiveness and longer-term sustainability.

units of subnational governments—to "benefit jurisdictions"—thus permitting the level and mix of such services to vary according to local preferences. If local benefit jurisdictions are to perform this role, they require information on local preferences. The benefit jurisdiction model would address this problem through taxes and elections. Arguing that consumers can be confronted with the costs of alternative levels of service through local taxes and have the opportunity to express their preferences (through tax referenda or more general elections), proponents conclude that benefit jurisdictions can approximate the efficiencies of a market in the allocation of local public services by "pricing" municipal services and relying on the local political process to clear the market.

The organizational implications of this framework are straightforward. Responsibility for discrete public services should be assigned to the level of government whose boundaries incorporate the affected beneficiaries. That level of government should then be assigned a corresponding pricing instrument—a tax with a corresponding incidence—with which to ascertain demand.

Although useful as a starting point, the benefit jurisdiction framework does not address directly certain behavioral and technical factors that appear to be important in practice. It assumes that local politicians, and the people who work for them, are solely interested in serving the interests of their constituents and that constituents have both the means and the incentives to make their interests known. It also assumes away certain practical considerations. It ignores the high administrative costs that would be associated with assigning each function of the public sector to a distinct unit of government with its own field administration. And it does not take into account economies of scale in service production and thus the potential conflict between an organizational solution that would be most responsive and one that would be most efficient in a technical sense.

The behavioral implications of alternative organizational arrangements are addressed in what has been called the new institutional economics. This is a field that explains the behavior of politicians as the rational pursuit of self interest—the behaviors required for advancement in a political career—and explains the behavior of bureaucrats, similarly, as a rational, self-interested response to the working rules that allocate rewards and costs within the organization (Ostrom, Schroeder, and Wynne 1992). Although the organizational implications of institutional economics are consistent with those of the benefit jurisdiction model, greater emphasis is placed on incentives, specifically on factors that would make political leaders more vulnerable to their constituents. Emphasis is placed on *specificity* in the definition of local government responsibilities, in order to permit constituents to have a basis on which to judge performance (Israel 1987), and on the terms and conditions on which mayors obtain access to revenue. Attention is also directed to such issues as whether the mayor is appointed or elected (and what sort of career trajectory confronts a successful—or unsuccessful—mayor) and the mechanisms by which interest groups can make their wishes known to local governments and exert pressure to have them fulfilled. This is elegantly summarized in Hirschman's concept of "exit and voice," in which he argues for organizational arrangements that offer consumers the option of either taking their business elsewhere (exit) or increasing their influence over providers through "voice"—enhancing the lines of communication between providers and constituents (Hirschman 1970).

Empirical evidence suggests that there are means of addressing the technical constraints in the benefit jurisdiction model. Urban services are not, and need not be, organized as sectoral autarkies, that is, as single-purpose, self-contained units of government, relying only on own-source revenue and executing their functions solely by force account. In practice, urban service delivery—particularly in the developed Western economies— is organized as a complex network of relationships between multipurpose units of local government, central governments, and private firms, where local governments serve as decisionmaking entities for some services and as executing agents of central governments for others and where private firms are involved in the execution of a wide variety of local public services on behalf of local government.

This complexity is desirable. It is helpful, first, in addressing the high administrative costs that would result from assigning each function of government to a separate public entity. A single tier of government can act in multiple capacities. Local government can act as the provider of local public services—as a benefit jurisdiction with respect to some services— while acting as an administrative agent of higher levels of government in others. In this respect, a single level of government can assume functional responsibility for multiple services, thus reducing the aggregate administrative costs of the public sector. The use of local governments in an agency role is widespread in the G-5 countries (France, Germany, Japan, the United Kingdom, and the United States). In the United States, for example, the federal government relies on local government to implement some of its major income distribution policies, including the administration of AFDC (Aid to Families with Dependent Children) and food stamps.

In many instances, the private sector has an important role to play in improving municipal service delivery. The benefits of economies of scale (as well as the incentive effects of private competition) can be captured with various forms of contracting out to private firms or even privatization of some services that are traditionally considered public. The distinction between the "provision" and "production" aspects of service delivery—a distinction between the government's role of deciding what type and quality of services is to be produced and the role of actually producing it—has long been recognized in both theory and practice (Musgrave and Musgrave 1984). This distinction is useful in addressing the apparent conflict between the demand responsiveness of decentralized decisionmaking and the presumed economies of scale of centralized production. As Silverman, among others, has recently noted, production can be organizationally separated from provision (Silverman 1992). Such a separation allows the benefits of local decisionmaking to be captured by assigning the provision role to local government, while allowing economies of scale to be captured by permitting larger entities of government or private firms to be responsible for production. This separation of provision from production is commonly observed in the G-5 countries, particularly in the execution of capital works. Although local governments play a large role in the delivery of infrastructure services in the G-5 countries, little construction is done by municipal employees. Major off-site capital works are typically constructed by private contracting firms. Residential infrastructure in industrial countries is almost entirely produced by private sector developers (prodded by local development regulations). The production of such services as water supply (in the case of France and the United Kingdom), solid waste management (in the United States), and bus transit is also assigned to private firms in the G-5. Box 3.2 illustrates some of the main options for private sector participation in urban infrastructure and describes some recent examples of private sector involvement in developing countries.

BOX 3.2 OPTIONS FOR PRIVATE SECTOR PARTICIPATION IN URBAN INFRASTRUCTURE

Finding the right balance of roles and responsibilities for municipal infrastructure between the public sector and the private sector depends on a number of factors that vary within each country. These include the existing performance of public sector agencies, the administrative capacity of the relevant local government to regulate private suppliers, the interest and capacity of the private sector, and the political consensus for private provision.

World Development Report 1994 (World Bank 1994) sets out a menu of four main options for the provision and production of infrastructure, illustrating possible points within a broad array of institutional alternatives:

Option A: Public ownership and public operation. Public provision by a government department, public enterprise, or parastatal authority is the most common form of ownership and operation of municipal infrastructure (especially for roads, water supply, and sanitation). Successful public entities are run on commercial principles and give

BOX 3.2 (CONTINUED)

managers control over operations and freedom from political interference, but they also hold managers accountable, sometimes by using performance agreements or management contracts. The well-performing enterprises or agencies also follow sound business practices and are subject to the same regulatory, labor law, accounting, and compensation standards and practices as private firms. Tariffs are set to cover costs, and any subsidies to the enterprise are given for specific services and in fixed amounts. The water authorities in Botswana and Togo, the highway authorities in Ghana and Sierra Leone, and the restructured road agency in Tanzania are positive examples of this approach. Public entities can also contract out specific services or activities (such as solid waste collection, facility and vehicle maintenance, invoicing, and meter reading) to private firms, as has been done with good results by the metropolitan sanitation authority of Santiago, Chile (EMOS). But few successful cases of option A persist, because they are vulnerable to changes in governmental support. Many public entities perform well for a time and then fall victim to political interference.

Option B: Public ownership and private operation. For infrastructure activities involving a natural monopoly, such as the construction and operation of a municipal piped water

and sewerage facility, public ownership with private operation can be an efficient alternative. In this arrangement, the local government (or a regional association of municipal governments) retains majority or full ownership of the assets but accords the right to operate the facility to a private party, preferably on the basis of a transparent process of competitive bidding. This approach, known as "competition *for* the market," is typically implemented through lease contracts (which cover the full operation and maintenance of publicly owned facilities) or concessions, which also delegate responsibility for construction and financing of new capacity. Arrangements between the owner (government) and the operator (firm) are set out in a contract that includes any regulatory provisions. The private operator typically assumes all commercial risk of operation and shares in investment risk under concessions. Leases or concessions are under way for the passenger railways in Buenos Aires, Argentina; for water supply in Buenos Aires and Guinea; and for port facilities in Colombia, Ghana, and the Philippines. Concessions also include contracts to build and operate new facilities under the build-operate-transfer arrangement and its variants. Proliferating in recent years, concessions to build and operate facilities include

(Box continues on the following page.)

BOX 3.2 (CONTINUED)

toll roads in China, Malaysia, and South Africa; power plants in Colombia, Guatemala, and Sri Lanka; water and sanitation facilities in Malaysia and Mexico; and telephone facilities in Indonesia, Sri Lanka, and Thailand. Each has brought private financing to support new investments.

Option C: Private ownership and private operation. The private ownership and operation of infrastructure facilities are increasing, both through new entry by private firms in infrastructure markets and through divestiture of public ownership of entire systems. Private ownership is straightforward for services such as urban bus transit, which can be provided competitively. Twenty-seven developing countries allow cellular telephone service to be competitively provided, and many others allow private firms to construct electricity-generating plants and sell power to the national power grid. Where competition among suppliers is possible, private ownership and operation require little or no economic regulation beyond that applied to all private firms. Sometimes, the necessary competition can also occur across sectors or modes, as between road and rail or between electricity and gas. Where competition is necessarily limited, or where providers need to have access to common infrastructure (such as transit terminals), some regulation of both private and public providers may be required to prevent the abuse of monopoly power.

Option D: Community provision. Community provision is most common for local, small-scale infrastructure, such as access roads, water supply, and sanitation serving a well-defined user group or residential area, and it often complements publicly provided services. Successful community provision requires user involvement in decisionmaking, especially to set priorities for expenditure so as to ensure an equitable and agreed sharing of the benefits and costs. Technical assistance, training, and compensation to service operators are also very important to sustain service provision. When these elements are present, community self-help programs can produce good results at low cost, as in the Orangi Project in Karachi, Pakistan, which mobilized a low-income neighborhood to construct, finance, and maintain waterborne sewers.

Overall, this suggests that a "good" arrangement for urban service delivery is likely to be complicated and only partly defined by the designation of responsibilities and revenue sources to particular units of government. It is an arrangement in which the interests of national political bodies and local interest groups will be incorporated in different ways, with municipal governments performing as agents of central government in some capacities and as independent decisionmaking bodies in others and with private firms acting as agents of local government in various respects. It is an arrangement in which what is important are not the organizational labels, but rather the relationships—the rules that govern the transactions—among the various entities.

A Typology of Intergovernmental Relations

Although the relations between units of government can be organized in a variety of ways, not all such arrangements work equally well. Examples from developing countries reveal a variety of suboptimal arrangements: situations where feedback from constituents is blocked, where responsibilities are ambiguous, or where the relationship between central government and local government is rife with perverse incentives. The following examples illustrate that institutional arrangements between units of government can go wrong in a number of different ways.

The intergovernmental relations of a country are difficult to know. The official rules—the legal framework—are at best only an indicator of the actual locus of decisionmaking power and the influences that bear on decisionmakers. It is useful, nevertheless, to attempt to articulate common patterns in intergovernmental relations to illustrate the variety of circumstances that exist.

Three patterns of problematic institutional arrangements are discernible. The first might be called the overcontrolled local sector, where subnational governments are in effect merely administrative arms of the central government. Its obverse is laissez-faire decentralization, in which each tier of subnational government is almost sovereign and competes with other levels of government. The third might be called the perversely regulated local sector, where local governments have some degree of autonomy, but where the relationship with central leadership is characterized by perverse incentives.

The Overcontrolled Local Sector

This is historically the classic pattern in developing countries. It has two typical characteristics. First, a very high proportion of total public expenditure is made directly by the central government (or in federal countries, by large states). Second, local government, even within its circumscribed expenditure role, functions largely as an administrative arm of the central

Figure 3.1   Local Share of Public Expenditure in Selected Countries

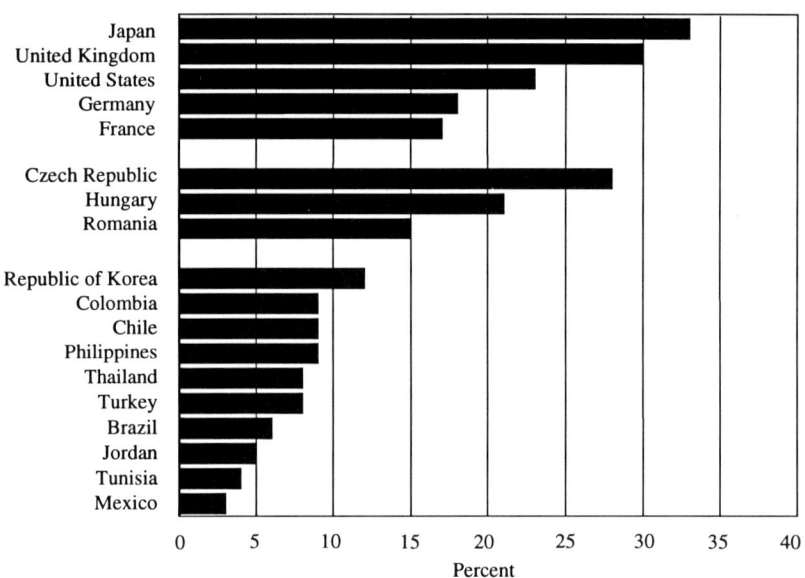

government, with the central government appointing the municipal executive and dictating virtually all expenditure and revenue decisions. This
approach to local government management starts with a laudable objective:
avoiding abuse of power at the local level, particularly important in a fluid
political environment with very uneven distribution of wealth and power
locally. However, this approach can fail because it emphasizes regulation
to such an extent that local autonomy and accountability are seriously
compromised.

Central government's dominance of total public sector expenditure is a
common pattern in developing countries. The local share of total public
sector expenditure in developing countries—even large countries such as
Mexico—is well under 10 percent (see figure 3.1). This is in contrast to the
G-5 countries, where the local share ranges from 17 percent (France) to 33
percent (Japan).[3]

Local governments in these countries, moreover, bear no resemblance
to autonomous political entities envisioned in the public finance literature.
To begin with, central governments, rather than local voters, choose the

municipal political executive. (Elected councils are often permitted but function in a purely advisory role.) Direct appointment of municipal executives is still the pattern in many large developing-country cities (see table 3.1). Elsewhere, central control over local political outcomes is discretionary but is widely used. In India, for example, state governments possess the legal authority to dismiss mayors whose performance they find unsatisfactory. Since independence, at any given time, 40 to 50 percent of the local authorities have been under state supersession.[4]

Central governments also directly control the allocation of municipal expenditure in this group of countries. Personnel is typically the largest single item of local government expenditure, and the ability of local government to recruit, retain, and motivate staff is critical to its ability to provide municipal services efficiently. In many developing countries, control over local personnel management decisions rests with central government. Central governments often control the number of positions local governments are allowed to maintain at each grade, the starting salaries and pay differentials between grades, the level of cost of living increases, and the appeals process for dismissal. In Turkey, for example, the staff list of each municipality is fixed by the government, along with the corresponding salary scale. Any amendments to the staff list have to be approved

Table 3.1 Structure of Political Accountability in Major Developing-Country Cities

City	Mayor	Council
Bombay, India	Directly elected	Temporarily dissolved
Jakarta, Indonesia	Appointed by government	Directly elected, no legislative power
Mexico D.F., Mexico	Appointed by government	Directly elected, no legislative power
São Paulo, Brazil	Directly elected	Directly elected at large, legislative power
Seoul, Rep. of Korea	Appointed by government	Directly elected, no legislative power
Budapest, Hungary	Directly elected	Elected: one-quarter directly by district; three-quarters at large by party list
Lagos, Nigeria	Directly elected	Elected
Shanghai, China	Elected by council	Elected

by the central government in a laborious process involving the Ministry of Interior, the State Personnel Organization, and the Council of Ministers. In some countries, central governments are directly involved in individual recruitment and promotion decisions. In Ghana, for example, local government staff are directly recruited, promoted, and paid by sectoral ministries of the central government. In the Philippines, municipal treasurers and tax assessors (until the recent reforms) were directly recruited, supervised, and paid by the central government's Ministry of Finance. In Indonesia, all full-time staffing positions are subject to central government recruitment and promotion and are paid directly by central government.

Central governments also control the sectoral composition and size of local government budgets. In Morocco, for example, each municipality's budget must be approved by the Ministry of Interior before the funds can be disbursed against it—an approval process that includes a verification that all centrally mandated expenditures are in the budget and a verification that personnel expenditure aggregates agree with the *Loi de Cadres* for each year (that is, the payroll of authorized grades and positions) and with the treasury allocation for municipal personnel expenditures. In Senegal, similarly, the annual budget review process includes a line-by-line negotiation of the expenditure estimates of each local authority. In the Philippines (until the recent reforms), the overall size of each local government's budget was determined by the local representative of the finance ministry. In addition, central budget regulations required that municipalities allocate 20 percent of their revenue sharing for development projects approved by the government; allocate 18 and 5 percent of their general fund for the national police and aid to hospitals within the province, respectively; and limit the proportion of the budget spent on personnel to 45 percent. An internal World Bank report estimated that an average of 46 percent of all local expenditures in the Philippines were made under central government mandate.

Municipal revenue levels are also regulated. In five of the eight developing-country cities listed in table 3.2, for example, local governments have no discretion over the rate of their principal tax. Governments use this control to keep the rates of local taxes extremely low. In Jakarta, for example, the government of Indonesia limits the property tax rate to 0.1 percent of assessed value. Even where local governments have some nominal discretion over the rate, central governments control the factors that determine how much these sources yield. In the Philippines, municipal governments are permitted to impose a property tax of between 0.5 and 2.0 percent of assessed value, but the regulations governing assessments are such that the maximum effective rate is less than one-tenth of 1 percent of

Table 3.2   Sources of Tax Revenue in Major Developing-Country Cities

City	Largest local tax			Other major tax	
	Name	Rate control	Percentage of tax revenue	Name	Percentage of tax revenue
Bombay, India	Octroi	Local	66	Property	13
Budapest, Hungary	Income	Central	95		
Jakarta, Indonesia	Automobile[a]	Central	72	Property	11
Lagos, Nigeria	Property	Local	90		
Mexico, D.F., Mexico	Payroll	Central	58	Property	21
São Paolo, Brazil	Services	Local	80	Property	17
Seoul, Rep. of Korea	Property	Central	25	Tobacco	21
Shanghai, China	Business profit[b]	Central	50	Industry	30

a. Includes separate taxes on purchase and ownership.
b. Amount to be shared with central government is negotiated.
Source: Municipal budgets.

market value. In India, the combination of state-imposed rent control and Supreme Court interpretations of property tax legislation has resulted in the virtual exemption of all but the city's most recently constructed housing stock. In Mexico, in an environment in which annual inflation has been as high as 150 percent, local governments are forbidden to adjust assessments for inflation unless they obtain the simultaneous concurrence of the mayor, the council, the governor, and the state legislature.

The performance of overcontrolled systems has not been evaluated systematically. Max Weber's classic work on organization argued that the centralized, vertically integrated bureaucracy is in fact the most efficient form of organization (Weber 1964). But there is good evidence that concentrating so large a proportion of expenditure decisions in the hands of ministers whose constituencies are national, and permitting so few channels of demand expression through local political leadership, makes it difficult to respond to local constituents. The problem is particularly acute where the central government's revenue structure is also centralized (with heavy reliance on indirect taxes and little use of user charges) and thus is cut off from price-related indicators of demand. Also, as one observer of the local political scene has noted, "The practice of appointing municipal executives has often resulted in the mayor's position being held by individuals with only short-term interests in municipal affairs. Where careers are dependent on the fortunes of political sponsors, officials are more likely to adhere to national policies at the expense of local circumstances" (Lowder 1986).

Typically the administrative demands of this tight system of regulation overload the administrative abilities of the public sector in some developing countries. Central governments thus find that they lack the information required to exercise this control intelligently. In Turkey, for example, governors are permitted one week to approve or modify a budget once it has been passed by the municipal council. Approval is therefore virtually automatic. The fact that revenue estimates have been inflated unrealistically to satisfy the central budgetary regulations goes unexamined. In Kenya, similarly, the Ministry of Local Government is required to approve or modify all local budgets before the commencement of the fiscal year but lacks the basic information (such as data on actual income and expenditures for any previous year) on which to base its approvals. Under these conditions, the overcentralized system is perhaps the worst of both worlds, in the sense that there is neither a clear bureaucratic chain of command nor a clearly defined scope of local discretion. Central regulation then merely obfuscates responsibility.

Laissez-faire Decentralization

The obverse case is laissez-faire decentralization, in which there are multiple levels of government, each with political autonomy and financial autonomy over expenditure and revenue, but without any clearly defined functional responsibility. Again, this type of system can arise as a result of good intentions—typically the desire to devolve power to local governments.

Brazil is perhaps the extreme example of this pattern. Brazilian *municipios* have historically enjoyed complete political autonomy, with councils and mayors chosen through competitive local elections (except during a short interruption during the military regime of the 1960s). They have complete expenditure autonomy and freedom over the rates of the taxes that have been assigned to them. When the extremely productive value added tax was introduced (at the state level) in Brazil, the municipios were assigned a fixed 20 percent share of the proceeds, without restrictions on its use. Brazilian legislation, while designating an extensive list of functions in which municipal government may choose to act, assigns the same functions concurrently to state government. While functions such as the national defense are assigned to the federal government, major public sector activities, including education, health, and the provision of urban infrastructure, are assigned concurrently to all three levels of government, with no clear definition of their respective roles. (Only one function—

natural gas—is exclusively assigned to the state level; and only one—urban transport—is assigned primarily to municipalities.) As a result, both state and municipal governments may operate primary schools, health services, road construction and maintenance programs, or any other public service simultaneously within the same jurisdiction. In Brazil, the de facto division of labor between levels of government reflects a pattern of historical bargains and ongoing negotiations.

Again, the impact of this arrangement on the efficiency and responsiveness of urban service delivery has not been systematically assessed, but the evidence points to the operation of two kinds of perverse incentives in these systems. First, it would seem to obscure the accountability of local governments to their constituents. Without clearly defined functional responsibilities, local government could not easily be held responsible by their constituents for the outcomes of any particular services. Second, it would seem to set up a perverse set of relationships between local government politicians and their counterparts at the state (and central government) level. Without a clear distinction between the functions of each tier—in effect, without a hard budget constraint on the extent of state participation in functions that a mayor is under pressure to provide—the extent of state participation is likely to be determined through bargaining. Where state government resources are allocated on this basis, they are likely to reflect neither the priorities of local consumers nor those of the state government, but rather the lobbying skills of local politicians.

The Perversely Regulated Local Sector

Although Brazil is an extreme example, it provides the polar case for the set of intermediate cases that constitute the more prevalent pattern: countries in which there is some degree (de facto if not de jure) of local political autonomy and some (de jure) assignment of functional responsibilities, but where there is a built-in vertical gap—a lack of correspondence between the revenue authority of local government and its expenditure responsibilities—that is addressed in undesirable ways.

There are two undesirable ways in which the vertical gap is closed. Perhaps the most common is through direct, but ad hoc, expenditures by central government ministries. The practice of direct intervention by central ministries is often the legacy of past crises. As Lowder describes it, central intervention is often provoked by disasters—outbreaks of communicable disease, for example—and the perceived failure of local government to respond. "In response to these crises, specialized technical agencies are introduced to manage utilities such as potable water, electricity, housing for the poor . . . these are usually autonomous or responsible directly to a minister, and empowered to override both the spheres of action and the territorial jurisdiction of other authorities" (Lowder 1986). In South Asia, the government's intervention has tended to be permanent. Central (or in India, state) public works ministries and development authorities take on responsibility for municipal capital works, leaving only the task of operations and maintenance to local government. In Latin America, the participation is more ad hoc. In Venezuela, for example, although municipal governments have the legal responsibility to provide water supply, sewerage, urban roads, and power distribution, agencies of the central government intervene in the provision of these services at will (and in fact account for the vast majority of public sector expenditure on these services).

The problem with this type of intervention is not its objective—avoiding local service failures—but rather the pattern of open-ended participation by central government ministries, which tends to set up the same perverse incentives as prevail in the laissez-faire model. Constituents have difficulty holding local governments accountable for any specific function, and the mayor is encouraged to act as a lobbyist before the central government ministries, rather than as an individual ultimately responsible for specific functions. The more stable South Asian approach contributes an additional nuance. With responsibility for capital investment assigned to state agencies, but operations and maintenance left to the municipal level, disputes over debt liabilities and refusals to assume maintenance obligations on new assets are common. Given the revenue advantage that states have over local governments, overspending on investments (relative to operations and maintenance) is also characteristic of South Asia.

Countries also fill the vertical gap through intergovernmental transfers. As described in chapter 4, transfers have an important role in virtually any system of multitiered government finance. The problem is not transfers per se, but the terms and conditions on which transfers are provided. Intergovernmental transfers take various undesirable forms. First, in some countries, the level of transfers is itself unpredictable or determined largely by negotiation. In Kenya, for example, the central government is legally obligated to make an annual payment to local government in lieu of property taxes owed on government-owned property. It has often failed to do so, which has set off a cycle of mutual default, such that local governments no longer service their debt to the government loans authority, the government hospitals fail to pay their bills to the municipal water authorities, and the water authorities refuse to pay their income taxes to the government.

**BOX 3.3 CONTRASTING
APPROACHES TO CAPITAL
ALLOCATION: PAKISTAN
AND MEXICO**

Pakistan's Annual Development Plan (ADP) process typifies a highly centralized system, which permits every project to be evaluated in the light of the nation's investment priorities and the availability of financing. It results, however, in project selections being made by people far removed from the beneficiaries, with little information about projects and less idea of beneficiary priorities. The ADP process begins with a municipality's submission of a project proposal to the provincial government, where it is subjected to technical review; if technically approved, it is then included in a larger pool of projects eligible for financing. Financing decisions are made annually and begin with an estimate of overall resource availability by the central government's Ministry of Finance. Once an overall division of funds between government and provinces is made, the provincial government tentatively matches resources with projects; it then forwards its recommendations to the central government's annual plan coordinating committee, which approves the size and sectoral allocation of the overall package and submits it to the national economic council, presided over by the president. This lengthy process successfully eliminates technically unsound projects and matches resources to projects, but it incorporates no mechanism for weighing the degree of local commitment to investment projects.

Mexico's National Solidarity Program (PRONASOL) represents only the current stage in Mexico's gradual process of decentralizing its project allocation system (starting from a system in which 94 percent of public sector capital investment decisions were made by sectoral ministries at the federal level). The program is funded from an earmarked share of the national budget (carved out of what used to be sectoral ministry budgets). The share of funds allocated to each state tends to reflect the economic and political priorities of the federal government. But within each state, the allocation of funds among projects draws on a well-developed system of negotiation between the mayor and community groups, in which PRONASOL funding is made conditional on the community's willingness to provide counterpart contributions in cash or in kind. Although mayors have the latitude to vary the terms of each project agreement, the matching requirement is universal. PRONASOL, as a grant program, still embodies interjurisdictional subsidies, but the explicit inclusion of mayors in the allocation process and the program's use of counterpart matching contribution as a rationing device are significant reforms.

Even where recurrent transfers are distributed according to formula, transfers may have perverse incentive effects. "Dearness allowances" in some Indian states and the Subsidi Daerah Otonomi grants in Indonesia both fund part or all of local personnel costs, for example. This encourages local governments to lobby for more positions, regardless of need. Transfers based on the size of revenue gaps similarly encourage municipal governments to exaggerate expenditures or reduce local tax effort. In Morocco, for example, the size of a municipality's transfer is based on the gap between its estimated revenues and expenditures. Although both revenue and expenditure estimates must be approved by government—limiting the scope for local strategic behavior—debt service is automatically included as an element in approved expenditure. Even unconditional transfers, like Brazil's, may embody arbitrary interjurisdictional subsidies. Brazil's largest municipal transfer, a 25 percent share of the value added tax, is distributed largely on the basis of the "origin" of value added tax collections—that is, at the point of production, not at the point of consumption, where much of the incidence presumably falls. The result is a cross-subsidy from consumers throughout Brazil to the residents of industrial enclaves, a transfer that, for example, enables the municipio of São Bernardo (the site of Volkswagen do Brasil) to operate a municipal symphony, courtesy of Volkswagen buyers throughout the country.

In developing countries, transfers are also used to finance capital investment. And again, although this may be an appropriate role for central government (particularly where long-term capital markets are not well developed), the allocation mechanism for capital financing tends to be more responsive to the political interests of the central government than to local expressions of effective demand.

Capital allocation systems vary considerably among countries. In Pakistan, for example, the official system of capital allocation (see box 3.3) in principle permits every project to be evaluated on both technical and economic grounds, in the light of the nation's investment priorities and the availability of financing. It nevertheless results in project selections being made by people far removed from beneficiaries, with little information about projects and less idea of beneficiary priorities. The Mexican PRONASOL program, in contrast, is said to institutionalize a high degree of beneficiary involvement but tends to bypass the capital budgeting process of sectoral ministries at the central and state levels. In Turkey, the central government's public works agency, Iller Bank, is responsible for both financing and constructing municipal public works. Its investment choices, similarly, are said to reflect the technical preferences of its engineers and the interests of the central government.

CHAPTER FOUR

Directions for Reform

THE basis for making recommendations on the reform of inter-governmental relations does not point to strong and simple conclusions. Although the academic literature is useful conceptually, it is not specifically prescriptive. The approach of the industrial countries, which might be presumed to demonstrate successful models, provides some common sense of direction but is still one of considerable variety and frequent experimentation. The past experience from developing countries appears largely to be a source of negative lessons. The most relevant body of evidence is emerging from the countries that are now in the process of decentralization. But these reforms are still in their initial stages. There are no before-and-after cases of developing-country decentralization on which to base normative advice. The conclusions presented in this chapter are therefore subject to these limitations but serve to provide an overall sense of the direction for reform.

The evidence suggests that the reform of the structure of municipal service delivery has three elements: the clarification of functional responsibilities between levels of government, the authorization of revenue sources corresponding to functional responsibilities, and the institution of a system of accountability that encompasses both regulation by central government and incentives for responsiveness to local constituents.

Linking Services to Levels of Government

Clarity in the division of functional responsibilities between levels of government would appear to be an essential condition of any reform in the structure of urban service delivery. Judging from the institutional development literature and the anecdotal evidence from developing countries, a clear linkage between a unit of government and a specific service seems to be critical in enabling constituents to hold local governments accountable for specific functions. It is also useful in eliminating the soft budget constraint that encourages mayors to act as lobbyists before the central government ministries rather than as individuals ultimately responsible for the performance of specific services.

Where functional responsibilities are not well defined, clarifying them would appear to be the first priority for reform and an essential precondition for progress on the other two elements of reform. There can be no correspondence between revenue and expenditure assignments unless expenditure responsibilities are known. And any attempt to improve accountability through regulation and constituent access is undermined when the function for which the entity is responsible is not defined.

Clarity is not achieved by a mere act of legislation, that is, a constitutional demarcation of functions between tiers of government. The developing world is full of such documents, and they are routinely ignored or violated. Clarity, above all, requires that central government refrain from ad hoc interventions in responsibilities that have been nominally assigned to local government and that it observe the hard budget constraint with respect to local functions, no matter how disagreeable the outcomes. And this, in turn, requires a structure of subnational government that renders such ad hoc interventions unnecessary and obviates the crises that provoke central government intervention.[1]

Assigning functional responsibilities to local governments does not mean that they must be direct producers of the services in question. As mentioned earlier, local governments can benefit from contracting out or privatizing some of the services they have responsibility for providing. This approach can increase efficiency and improve quality and reliability of services, and it offers much-needed flexibility for small municipalities and for countries where local-level government capacity is particularly weak. A detailed framework for identifying the options for private sector involvement in urban infrastructure is outlined by Kessides (1993a).

Effective devolution of responsibilities to local governments requires, among other things, a system of revenue assignment and budgetary discretion that permits them to perform the roles that have been assigned to them.

But it may first require governments to legislate more geographic specificity into their municipal organic laws. Metropolitan areas are a special,
more complex case (see box 4.1). Although they constitute an important
practical policy issue, appropriate institutional arrangements tailored to
the complexities of metropolitan management are beyond the scope of this
book. One of the traditional justifications for the lack of any rigid division
of functions between government levels is the great variety of circumstances in which local government operates, that is, the concern that a rigid
division of functions—a hard budget constraint applied to all situations—
would work to the detriment of poor, weak, or otherwise exceptional,
jurisdictions.

In some countries, the organic laws governing local government are a
cause of, rather than a solution to, this problem. The organic laws of many
developing countries fail to recognize the different circumstances of different jurisdictions, making no distinction between urban or rural municipalities or between urban municipalities of different sizes. In Brazil, for
example, the rules that apply to São Paulo (population: 11.2 million) apply
equally to Pirapora de Bom Jesus (population: 4,585). Similarly, Chile,
Colombia, and Mexico all make no distinctions between urban and rural
areas or between urban areas of different sizes in the formal structure of
local government. (The one-size-fits-all approach is also used in some
Anglophone African countries—Ghana and Nigeria, for example.) Under
these conditions, functional specificity is difficult. The functions, such as
secondary education, that could comfortably be assigned to the municipal
governments of large metropolitan areas cannot be so assigned, because
they cannot also be performed by the governments of tiny villages.

Geographic distinctions are already made in some parts of the world.
The enabling laws of subnational governments in most of the Maghreb and
South Asia, for example, make legal distinctions between urban and rural
government and provide for varying degrees of autonomy for cities of
different sizes. In India, however, the graduation process appears to lag
behind the rate of urban growth: places that were villages at thc time of
their initial designation are now cities but retain the limitations of their
former status. Geographic distinctions are also characteristic of the
industrial countries. In the British structure, the full line of municipal
services in metropolitan areas is assigned to district governments. In
nonmetropolitan areas, services that are needed in both urban and rural
areas (education, personal social services, police and fire protection)
are provided by county governments. Those that are specifically urban
(housing, public transport, refuse collection) are assigned to separate
urban (district) governments. The German structure of local government,

**BOX 4.1 THE SPECIAL CASE OF
METROPOLITAN MANAGEMENT**

Metropolitan areas present special challenges in the management of local public services for two important reasons. First, their size dictates the need for multiple jurisdictions. This defining characteristic introduces significant complications in applying three basic principles: the unambiguous assignment of functions, the linking of financing authority with functional responsibility, and accountability. Second, metropolitan areas usually represent substantial political and economic power that is capable of creating major distortions in central-local relationships and among municipalities.

Nevertheless, good metropolitan management requires the application of the three guiding principles to a heightened degree if the consequences of ambiguity, overlap, confusion, and discontinuity in service management are to be avoided. However, other crucial principles would need to be incorporated into the difficult process of putting the cardinal principles into practice. Agreement on functional responsibilities would need negotiations laterally among jurisdictions as well as vertically with higher levels of government. Benefit jurisdictions and spillovers would have to be determined for each type of service with a perspective of several contiguous local urban jurisdictions rather than just one. Where a service area must cross jurisdictional boundaries in order to be most beneficial to users, or most

protective of the public interest, the authority for managing the service needs to reside at the multijurisdictional level. Then, the critical requirement is to cede to a management entity the autonomy and authority to act effectively without losing accountability to jurisdictions; this is a manifestation of the problem that confronts central government in structuring its relationship with municipalities, with the interesting twist that power is being passed upward from the lower jurisdictions. Accountability of a multijurisdictional entity must go in two directions: to the jurisdictional bodies that authorize its existence and to the clients of the service it provides.

A frequent (and convenient) response to the complexity of multijurisdictional management is the creation of a metropolitan authority that becomes a superior government over several jurisdictions. This response is not necessarily a solution if it becomes apparent that benefit jurisdictions and paying jurisdictions are greatly at odds for a number of important services. However, the second key characteristic of metropolitan areas—their political and economic clout—is often used to dampen, at least for some time, the effects of these disparities. Metropolitan areas in developing countries are often able to command a disproportional share of central resources, usually in nontransparent ways. The extent to which other municipalities sense this to be the case increases the difficulty of establishing sound central-local relationships.

similarly, provides for a two-tier system of local government in nonmetropolitan areas, with combined responsibilities in large cities.

Linking Revenues to Expenditures

If a clear division of functional responsibilities is to be workable, local governments need to have the revenue authority to perform the responsibilities that have been assigned to them, without having to appeal for direct expenditure to central government. Although revenue reform does not imply a severance of intergovernmental transfers, it does imply the replacement of ad hoc grants with transfers based on clearly defined rules.

Finance Follows Function

The particular structure of local revenues—the mix of user charges, taxes, transfers, and loans—that is appropriate in a given context depends, first and foremost, on the functions that have been assigned to local government. Different kinds of revenue have different impacts on behavior and different patterns of incidence: user charges impose costs on individuals and can thereby ration consumption by price; benefit taxes can impose costs more broadly on the taxpayers within a jurisdiction but can only ration consumption through the local political process. Transfers make it possible to move money across jurisdictions, enabling central government to influence the behavior of local governments and to redistribute income between constituents of different local jurisdictions. The choice of instruments depends on the objectives that are being sought, and the objectives vary according to the function that is being financed.

User Charges

Where the benefits of a service are largely confined to individual consumers, and where there are no major adverse distributional consequences (and where it is administratively feasible), user charges are generally the most appropriate means of financing. In effect, user charges are a means of rationing consumption according to willingness to pay and a way to extract information about consumer preferences directly, by moving the consumption decision beyond the local government, directly to the consumer. To the extent that price can be varied with quantity, user charges can function as a pricing mechanism, confronting beneficiaries with a choice of different levels at appropriate prices and allowing individual consumers to decide on the quantity of a given service they want to consume based on their own tastes and preferences.

Piped water, bus transit, and toll roads, for example, are all services for which user charges are appropriate. Fees for refuse collection and sewerage are also appropriate.[2] Urban governments in developing countries in fact already impose such charges, but the level of charges is typically far below what it should be, either in terms of the financial costs of providing the service, economic costs or users' willingness to pay. (As a result, in the Federal District of Mexico, for example, subsidies to the municipal bus line consume about 22 percent of the district's recurrent budget.) The constraint on the present use of user charges is partly regulatory. Central governments restrict the level of user charges, ostensibly on distributional grounds. This justification does not hold up to scrutiny. Subsidies for water supply or bus transit are particularly ineffective means of pursuing poverty reduction goals (because they inadvertently and often preferentially subsidize consumers who are not poor) and are inefficient (because they reward overconsumption). Analysts of both water utilities and bus companies also note the adverse management implications of such subsidies. Because governments rarely provide full compensation to the providers for the full costs of these subsidies, their costs take the form of deferred maintenance and reluctance to extend service into low-income areas.

Central governments can therefore encourage the use of user charges through deregulation. But the evidence from developing countries suggests that municipal governments will not use this revenue source efficiently, even where they have the legal authority to do so, as long as less politically sensitive revenue sources are available. As discussed below, user charge reform must therefore be synchronized with reform in the other sources of municipal revenue.

Benefit Taxes

Local taxes are generally an appropriate means of financing services whose benefits, though not confined to individual consumers, are nonetheless localized. Yet the benefits do not extend beyond the municipal boundaries. In a sense, local taxes are the collective analog of user charges. Where user charges are the means by which individuals can express their demand for services whose benefits are largely private, local taxes are the means by which taxpayers within a community can express their demand for services that are consumed collectively. Benefit taxes also provide a degree of geographical equity to the financing of municipal services, imposing the costs of municipal services on the people who benefit from them.

Virtually all countries already assign some form of local tax to their local governments (see table 4.1). Reform therefore consists in part of

Table 4.1 Municipal Lending Organizations

Country/ organization	Organizational form	Source of funds	Portfolio results	Collateral	Share of total capital transfer
Brazil: PRAM	Managed by unit of state planning secretariat; state bank acts as financial agent	IBRD and state; capitalized to revolve	Good	Withholding from transfers	Large only in small towns
Colombia: FINDETER	Loans originated by private banks; rediscounted by fund administered by the board	Government equity, retained earnings, IDB, IBRD loans	Good	Borrower pledges transfers, specific source	Small
Morocco: FEC	Board comprised of representatives of ministries of interior and finance, Banque Al-Maghreb, and other government agencies	Bonds floated by Caisse Central de Garantie, external aid and lending institutions, government capital	Good	Indirectly financed through government transfers	Small
Indonesia: RDA	Account in Ministry of Finance	Government loans	Poor	None	Small
Jordan CVDB	Legally independent board, chaired by minister	Compulsory local government deposits, central bank loans, external aid and lending institutions	Poor	Withholding from transfers	Large, but local governments have few functions
Kenya: LGLA	Legally independent board, chaired by minister	Donor onlending	Poor	None	Large in small local governments

overcoming the regulatory and administrative constraints on the use of these taxes. As noted earlier, local taxation is often highly regulated, with central government controlling rates and exemption policies and any other factors that affect the level of tax liabilities. Like the controls on user charges, this degree of regulation does not appear to be justified (at least on distributional or fiscal grounds). Although governments are justified in restricting the *kind* of taxes municipal governments may impose (in order to prevent local governments from exporting their tax burdens onto neighboring jurisdictions), there does not appear to be a justification for a central government preventing a municipal jurisdiction from choosing the "price" of services financed indirectly through taxation.[3]

Local tax deregulation can involve the removal of explicit controls on tax rates. It can also include the removal of more subtle restrictions on tax yields. In countries with high levels of inflation, one of the major constraints on the yields of the property tax is the stipulation that properties may not be revalued without a physical inspection. Indexation is the solution to this problem. (Some states in Mexico, for example, now permit automatic adjustments in property valuations based on a cost of living index.)

Reform may also require a change in the mix of benefit taxes that local governments are permitted to impose, to encourage the use of more easily administered, less politically sensitive taxes. There are no perfect local taxes (see box 4.2). The factors that make for a good benefit tax—a broad base, with direct incidence—also make for difficult administration.

BOX 4.2 CHOOSING AMONG LOCAL BENEFIT TAXES

Property taxes. The property tax is the most universally assigned local tax but rarely stands alone. Among the eight major developing-country cities listed in table 4.1, for example, the property tax is assigned to six but is the principal source of revenue in only two. As a local incidence tax, the property tax performs well: the incidence of the tax (at least its residential component) is geographically confined, and its coverage is broad enough to reach the majority of beneficiaries. The property tax is, however, difficult to administer successfully. In part, the reasons are technical: the number of tax-paying units is large. Assess-

ments are inherently controversial because values must be imputed, rather than observed from actual transactions, and the base must be revalued annually to maintain its buoyancy. (Conditions in developing countries make the property tax particularly difficult to administer—the basic market data on which the property assessments are based are inaccessible or unreliable.) But there are also particular political costs associated with the property tax: as a direct tax, its burden is especially visible; and as a tax on wealth, its burden falls disproportionately on groups with great political influence.

Income and payroll taxes. Local income and payroll taxes are not uncommon in developing countries.

BOX 4.2 (CONTINUED)

(Of the eight cities in table 4.1, two— Budapest and Mexico—derive income from this source.) Various forms of local income taxes are also imposed in countries as disparate as Kenya and Sweden. Personal income taxes have the geographically defined incidence sought in a benefit tax, and where imposed in conjunction with a national income tax (as in Budapest), they are cheap to administer. The ability of income taxes to function as prices is constrained by their narrow coverage. In low-income countries, income taxes that are confined to formal sector employment fall on too small a proportion of the population to serve effectively as benefit taxes: they impose costs on too small a proportion of beneficiaries. In Kenya, for example, the local payroll tax is in effect a tax on public schoolteachers' salaries, except in Nairobi. Developing countries employ more rudimentary forms of income taxation, including flat poll taxes and taxes based on imputed income. But income taxes that attempt to reach incomes in the informal sector are often not cost-effective to administer. (In Onitsha, Nigeria, the costs of administering the poll tax exceed the entire revenues of the tax.) Income and payroll taxes are therefore more suited to higher-income countries where coverage is broader.

Utility taxes. Taxes imposed in connection with utility bills, particularly with electricity bills, are also not uncommon in developing countries. Shanghai derives a significant share of its tax revenue from a surcharge on electricity bills. In Jordan, a flat fee (earmarked for garbage collection) is imposed as part of the residential electricity bill. In principle, such taxes have localized incidence and, given the ubiquity of electric service even in illegal settlements, reasonably broad coverage. Costs of administration are low, as the tax can be imposed jointly with electricity bills. The extent to which an electricity surcharge can be relied upon exclusively is limited, however, by the basis of assessment: if the tax is imposed ad valorem (as in Shanghai), it distorts the price of power. If it is imposed as a flat fee (as in Jordan), it fails to capture variations in ability to pay (and is therefore limited by the tax-paying ability of the poorest electricity consumers).

Taxes on automobiles. Local automobile taxes—both recurrent taxes on automobile ownership and one-time taxes on purchase— are also significant auxiliary sources of revenue. Automobile taxes are the primary tax source in Jakarta, where two separate taxes— one on purchases, the other on sales—contribute 22 percent and 14 percent of municipal tax revenues, respectively. Except in multijurisdictional metropolitan areas, the incidence of these taxes is easy to confine. Automobile taxes are relatively easy to administer and enforce.

Countries exacerbate the administrative problem by assigning too many benefit taxes to their local governments (each with its own separate administrative overhead). The number should be reduced. As a country's economy modernizes, with an increasing proportion of income earned through formal sector employment, there may also be a case for increasing reliance on personal income taxes (following the model of the northern European countries and Japan).

Reform of Transfers

Any attempt to improve urban service delivery must address the largest source of local revenue, intergovernmental transfers. Transfers can serve several important positive roles in the financing of municipal services. First, they permit central governments to influence the sectoral pattern of local expenditure—to use the power of the purse to induce local governments to undertake expenditures that are of national rather than local interest, compensating local government for the costs of services that the central government expects them to provide. Left to their own devices, local governments would be expected to base their budget decisions only on the benefits captured by their constituents; transfers can induce local governments to take wider, national benefits into account.

Second, transfers permit central governments to use local governments as agents of national income redistribution policies. Local governments themselves are badly positioned to pursue distributional objectives from their own tax bases. Poverty is not uniformly distributed in geographic terms: mayors in poor jurisdictions cannot redistribute income from high-income populations who live elsewhere. Central governments, with their ability to raise taxes from the high-income populations regardless of residence, can use intergovernmental transfers as a tool of national income distribution policy.[4]

Intergovernmental transfers are therefore appropriate wherever the central government expects local governments to make an expenditure on its behalf, on either sectoral or distributional grounds (and where it lacks the leverage to mandate the expenditure through regulation). But reform of transfers is required both to increase their effectiveness in achieving their sectoral and distributional objectives and to reduce the adverse side effects of badly targeted or badly administered transfers.

Perhaps the most important measure developing countries can take is to reduce the unnecessary adverse side effects of existing transfer programs to reduce the uncertainty and bargaining that now accompany intergovernmental financial flows and to remove incentives for strategic behavior. Ecuador has recently replaced its system of ad hoc annual grants with a formula-based transfer system. Countries can also revise transfer formulas to remove more subtle unintentional inducements to perverse behavior. Morocco is in the process of replacing its deficit-filling grant distribution formula with one based largely on population. Countries can also revise transfer formulas to reduce the extent of the arbitrary interjurisdictional transfers that are embedded in some transfer formulas. Brazil has recently moved to reduce the mandated "origin" content in its value added transfer formula, allowing states to increase the weight attached to factors such as population.

But countries also need to design transfer programs to finance adequately the expenditures they have assigned to local government. Large recurrent transfer systems are likely to be appropriate wherever services with major distributional or benefit spillover implications are assigned to local government. Primary education, for example, is an appropriate object of intergovernmental finance. The case for education transfers is most easily made on distributional grounds: primary education is arguably the largest transfer in kind to low-income populations that the public sector makes, and it is reasonably cost-effective, because wealthy people often do not send their children to public schools (Haddad and others 1990). There is a similar case for transfers that finance certain aspects of health care. Although there are few benefit spillovers from curative health care, there are clearly positive benefit spillovers from preventive health—the control of communicable diseases (health inspection, vector abatement, vaccinations for communicable diseases)—whose impacts spill across jurisdictional boundaries (Over 1991). And (as with education), there are distributional arguments for transfer financing both preventive and curative health care, on the grounds that publicly provided health care constitutes a reasonably cost-effective transfer in kind to low-income populations. In most of the G-5 countries, local government expenditures on primary education and primary health care are largely financed through intergovernmental transfers (originating at the national level in France and the United Kingdom and at the state or prefecture level in Germany and Japan).[5] There is also clearly a case for intergovernmental transfers to local governments to finance direct payments to the indigent. (Practices vary in the G-5 countries, with central governments making direct payments to indigent households in some cases and using local governments as agents in others. Both approaches are used in the United States.)

The effectiveness of transfers in achieving these objectives can, in principle, be increased through changes in design, that is, changes in the method used to determine the amount to be transferred, the criteria used to distribute the pool that can be distributed, and the conditions attached to use of the transfer. Where the intent of a transfer is to encourage increased expenditure on education, for example, there is a case for earmarking the transfer for this function (and for imposing a matching condition to ensure that recipient local governments do not reduce the expenditure they would otherwise have made on this function and substitute the transfer). Similarly, where the intent is to provide direct aid to low-income households, there is a case for making greater use of earmarking and matching.

Earmarking and matching are used in the G-5 countries, although more widely in the United States than in Europe or Japan. (Although transfer formulas in Japan and the United Kingdom are based on complex calculations of expenditure needs—local school enrollments and numbers of indigent households—no explicit conditionality is imposed requiring transferred funds to be spent accordingly.) The ability of developing-country governments to use similar techniques to improve the targeting of transfers depends on whether they also possess a similar quality of information on local revenue and expenditure and a similar capacity to monitor transfer use. In order to ensure that money is spent on functions of national interest, a government must have the capacity to ascertain and monitor local expenditures. To determine the level of subsidy required to achieve a desired level of expenditure, it must have data on relative strengths of local tax bases. G-5 countries possess this information. Central governments in developing countries do not. (In Nigeria, for example, even data on the population of localities were not available for many years, and few local governments can present an accurate statement of income and expenditure.) In consequence, countries may have to consider whether the direct provision of education or health services through central government ministries would be more cost-effective than attempts to encourage local officials to achieve the desired level of expenditure on these functions.

Access to Capital

Reform is also needed in the arrangements by which municipal governments obtain access to financing for capital investment in order to reduce arbitrariness in capital allocation, improve targeting, and (in South Asia) address the problems arising from the organizational separation of capital expenditure responsibility from operations and maintenance responsibility.

To an extent, improvements in allocation can be achieved by improving the targeting of grant programs. Grant reform is particularly appropriate in places where the preconditions for allocation by lending do not exist: where the local revenue base is too precarious, where the local political time horizon is too short, or where the object of the capital work reflects national, rather than local, interest. Thus, there is a case for concentrating on grant reform in Mozambique or Nepal (both countries without a history of viable local government); and there is a case (historically) for grant reform in Mexico, where the short tenure of mayors (a single, three-year term), coupled with the high staff turnover that typically accompanies changes in administration, limits the time horizon of political leaders. There is also a case for concentrating on grant reform where the works to be financed are of national interest, such as schools or health posts, where local government, in effect, acts as an agent of national sector or distributional policy.

Where the benefits of a capital work are largely local, a principal focus of reform has been on reforming the allocation process by changing the *terms* on which funding is provided, replacing grant financing with loan financing. In principle, loan financing has several desirable attributes. Providing funds on a loan, rather than a grant, basis would appear to be a means of improving targeting and depoliticizing the allocation process. By allocating funds on the basis of beneficiaries' willingness to incur debt, lending would appear to force potential beneficiaries to reveal their degree of commitment to specific projects. Lending would presumably help to depoliticize the allocation process by placing a price on finance, rather than requiring the government to attempt to ration a free good. In practice, it also usually takes time and political will to ensure that loan-based systems function effectively in improving the allocation of central finance.

Although governments already administer such loan programs, their effectiveness in doing so has been questioned. It would appear that with the taxpayers ultimately bearing the financial risks of bad loans, the pressure on governments to use access to credit for political purposes—to allocate resources to politically favored jurisdictions and to ease up on debt service enforcement in such jurisdictions—is difficult to resist.

As a result, there is increasing interest, particularly among donors, in privatizing this role: in turning responsibility for the mobilization and allocation of long-term savings over to the private capital market. Such an arrangement would, in effect, require that municipal governments seek funding on the same footing as any private sector borrower. The private sector model would seem to have much to recommend it. With their own capital at risk, private lenders would seem less likely to make unsound loans and more likely to insist on repayment. But in many developing countries, given the level of private sector development, the private market's demonstrated interest in lending to local government without implicit or explicit subsidies is very limited. Long histories of macroeconomic instability have, in many countries, caused private savers to view long-term financial commitments of any kind as extremely risky. Government controls on the returns to savings often prevent risks from being compensated by commensurate rewards. Local governments, as political entities lacking readily marketable collateral, are typically viewed as unattractive to private capital. Thus, even in countries where local governments have the legal authority to borrow, private capital markets have not been a significant source of funds. In some middle-income countries and those with relatively well-developed financial sectors, there are indications that tapping private capital markets will become more important in the future. Establishing incentives for strong financial discipline in municipalities will support progress in this area.

Given private capital market limitations, the focus of reform has turned to organizational hybrids: institutions that attempt to combine the commercial incentives of private lenders with the financial backing of central governments. Under the general rubric of municipal credit institutions (MCIs), these organizations attempt to put an arm's length between government and the lending process, MCIs essentially isolate lending and loan administration in an entity that enjoys some legal and bureaucratic separation from the government budgeting process and establish clearer allocation and recovery rules to defend the organization from political interference, while still ultimately carrying the financial backing of the government.

MCIs take a variety of forms (table 4.1). The legal status of MCIs varies from programs administered by a government planning agency (Brazil's PRAM) to a legally independent board (Jordan's CVDB). Sources of funds vary from government loans (including on-lending of donor funds) to various forms of domestic resource mobilization (including compulsory deposits by local governments and relending of loan repayments). And although various administrative and managerial measures can increase the likelihood of their success (see box 4.3), two overall conclusions emerge from the experience of MCIs in developing countries. First, although organizing a lending program as an MCI may provide some protection against government political interference, it cannot prevent it. A determined government can interfere in the lending decisions of any bank it owns, regardless of the bank's legal structure. Thus, what matters most is not the organizational form, but rather government's commitment to the financial integrity of the MCI's operations. Second, the viability of any lending program depends on the health of its borrowers. MCIs are unlikely to thrive where local governments are not creditworthy or where economic conditions are unstable. Government attempts to establish MCIs must therefore be accompanied by

**BOX 4.3 IMPROVING THE
PERFORMANCE OF MCIs**

Municipal credit institutions (MCIs) have a long and successful record in Europe, both as funds—the British Public Works Loans Board, for example—and as banks—Credit Local de France. Their record in developing countries is uneven. MCIs are often established with the support of donors, and the operating terms and conditions agreed on frequently are not consistently implemented (particularly after funds have been disbursed) nor are they carried over into other channels of funding for municipal capital investment. Through a variety of grants and competing donor programs, governments often continue to send mixed signals to potential municipal borrowers. Many MCIs have thus remained financial enclaves: demonstration projects with limited impacts.

Experience suggests several organizational characteristics that increase the effectiveness of MCIs. First, the enabling legislation of an MCI should clearly segregate the financial role that the institution is intended to perform from other governmental developmental interests in project selection, leaving the MCI free to make lending decisions solely on financial criteria and forcing it to be accountable for its financial performance.

This statutory separation can be reinforced through the terms on which government funding to the MCI is provided. Funding for the MCI should be provided en bloc, rather than on an individual project basis, with governments holding MCIs accountable for their overall financial performance and conditioning further financial backing on satisfactory financial returns, but refraining from interfering with individual project decisions. Government's commitment to the financial integrity of the MCI can also be reflected in the composition of its board. A representative of the Ministry of Finance, for example, is a useful counterbalance to the influence of a local government minister.

Internal administrative rules can also reduce political pressure on technical staff. Appraisal regulations should clearly define the terms and conditions under which loans will be approved, employing readily verifiable criteria (such as debt service coverage ratios) to assess the creditworthiness of potential borrowers and explicitly forbidding new loan commitments to jurisdictions that are currently in default.

If the MCI is to have a sustainable impact on the system of municipal credit allocation, governments must create the right kind of operating environment and incentives for the MCI. First, governments should refrain from undermining the market for MCI lending. They should not operate grant or soft loan programs that

(Box continues on the following page.)

directly compete with the markets the MCI is designed to serve because such competing programs, in effect, undermine the market for MCI lending and marginalize the MCI's impact. Second, governments should take the steps necessary to permit local governments to become good credit risks, including assigning revenue sources appropriate to local functional responsibilities and permitting greater autonomy over tax rates and expenditure decisions—credit institutions cannot be financially healthy when all their borrowers are ill.

MCIs should nevertheless be seen as a reasonable interim solution in many cases, a way station on the road to more direct relationships between municipal governments and private capital markets.

measures to support the financial health of municipal governments and the stability of the economy as a whole.

Ultimately, the existence of creditworthy local governments and a stable economic environment should provide the conditions for private lenders to enter this market, obviating the need for a government-backed municipal credit institution. This would allow countries to pursue the model increasingly used in industrial countries, in which local governments float bonds directly in the private capital market (as in the United States) or borrow from specialized lending institutions that operate without government backing. MCIs should therefore be seen as an interim solution, which can function as a way station on the road to more direct relationships between municipal governments and private capital markets.

Balancing Central Regulation with Local Accountability

The extent to which a system of municipal service delivery should rely on accountability upward to central government, through regulation, or downward to constituents is not an issue that lends itself to universal prescription. Whether central government bureaucrats or local systems of accountability are better stewards of public interest is not an issue that this book will resolve. Neither extreme appears to be desirable. Both forms of regulation are complementary. The role of local constituents in ensuring that the quality and mix of local services are appropriate has often been neglected. Nevertheless, as responsibilities are devolved to local government, some central regulation is still needed to ensure that local government behavior is consistent with national interests.

Central Regulation

Some degree of accountability to central government through a national regulatory framework appears to be appropriate to any structure of municipal service delivery. In no country are local governments entirely autonomous. In all the G-5 countries, as well as in developing countries, local governments function within a legal framework established in national (or in Germany and the United States, state) law. There is, nevertheless, a case for restraining the scope of central regulation in developing countries to issues where the behavior of local governments has adverse consequences outside their jurisdiction and where the central government has the administrative capacity to regulate effectively.

Central regulation is clearly appropriate where local government behavior can affect national policy. Thus, local governments should not have the authority to print money (a principle that was, in effect, violated by the provincial governments of Argentina under the previous regime). Central regulation on external borrowing by local governments is also appropriate in order to permit central control over the balance of payments. Central regulation over the aggregate level of domestic borrowing may also be justified. In the United Kingdom, for example, where local governments account for nearly half of public sector investment, the central government has historically attempted to control the aggregate level of local borrowing as an instrument of fiscal policy.

Central regulation is also clearly appropriate where local governments are carrying out functions on behalf of central government. As Winkler has pointed out in the case of education, even in the highly decentralized systems in some of the G-5 countries, central (or state) governments maintain control over certain policy decisions—the ages of mandatory attendance, the core curriculum—while relinquishing responsibility for day-to-day management to local government (Winkler 1991). As noted earlier, earmarking of intergovernmental transfers—a form of expenditure regulation—is clearly appropriate where the central government uses local government as an agent, in order to ensure that funds are spent in the manner the central government intends.

Systems of local accountability for purely local affairs are often desirable but take time to develop. In some cases, as a transitional measure, it may be necessary for central governments to exercise some oversight or regulatory control over local government affairs when local systems are

weak. But where the impact of local government behavior is largely localized, and regulation requires detailed knowledge of local conditions and
priorities, the case for central regulation is more difficult to justify. In such
cases, it is not clear that the regulations posed by central government are a
useful restraint.

Local Accountability

The obvious counterpart to central regulation is local accountability: local
constituents regulating the behavior of their political leaders and managers
of urban services. In Western countries especially, local elections are traditionally viewed as a key instrument for this purpose.[6] However, even in
countries with well-established electoral processes, supplementary measures are typically needed. The advent of local democracy, although increasingly common, is therefore no panacea.[7] Moreover, the view that
local elections always perform well in this role does not stand up to scrutiny.[8] The validity of elections in countries that have experienced long
periods of authoritarian rule appears particularly questionable. The reasons
for this are not all well understood. O'Donnell, Schmitter, and Whitehead
note that in such countries, "Voters will have relatively little experience in
choosing among candidates; party identification will be weak. . . . One can
therefore expect a good deal of tactical voting . . . [which may] be quite
disconnected from longer term class, sectoral, ethnic or other interests"
(O'Donnell, Schmitter, and Whitehead 1986). Lack of information, poor
communications, and the absence of strong traditions of community action
may also detract from the effectiveness of local elections.

There is nevertheless some evidence that specific changes in election
rules can influence the degree to which local elections function as referenda on local government performance. Venezuela has increased the local
focus of elections by changing the basis on which candidacies are identified. Until 1988, Venezuela's municipal elections were contested on the
basis of national party slates, rather than as individual candidacies, and the
winning party was permitted to designate its candidate for mayoral
positions after the elections. Candidates now run as individuals, a reform
that has reportedly shifted the focus of the campaign to more localized
issues.

Probably of more immediate relevance in a wide range of developing
countries are the alternative, and supplementary, means of holding local
municipal leaders accountable. Although there are no simple formulas,
many local governments could take measures to ensure more regular con-
sultations with constituents, develop stronger channels for monitoring the

satisfaction of users of local services, and link career progression of civil servants more strongly to their responsiveness to constituents. In the Republic of Korea, for example, mayors have traditionally been appointed by the government, but their career trajectories (determined by the Ministry of Home Affairs) are clearly based on their success in responding to local constituents. To this end, the city of Seoul operates "citizen complaint reporting centers," and the mayor and top administrative staff make themselves available every Saturday for a "day of dialog with the citizen." (As noted earlier, Korea has nevertheless introduced direct elections in all municipalities except Seoul.)

The geographic deconcentration of specific municipal services to submunicipal branch offices also appears to be a means of strengthening municipal accountability, because it brings providers into closer geographic proximity to clients. Such an arrangement is fairly common in large metropolitan areas. The Bombay Municipal Corporation is subdivided into four zones and twenty-three wards—headed by deputy municipal commissioners and ward councilors, respectively—with responsibility for solid waste removal, road maintenance, and water and sewerage services. Budapest is made up of twenty-two districts. Each district is headed by an elected mayor and has specifically assigned service responsibilities and independent revenue sources. Seoul, similarly, is divided into twenty-two Gu, each responsible for solid waste collection and street maintenance within its jurisdiction and authorized to charge a corresponding service fee.

In certain country contexts, a strong central audit function can bring to light information that can help to increase accountability. In France, for example, auditing of local government contracting has proved a useful tool in avoiding abuses by local authorities as decentralization has proceeded. However, audits function primarily as an input to a broader system of accountability. Unless the public interests that are meant to be served by the audit function are clearly articulated in the government system, the discipline that audits are supposed to impose can easily be subverted.

Synchronizing the Elements of Reform

There is clearly no one way to organize the delivery of urban services. The extent to which a system of accountability should rely on local politics or central regulation and the question of whether primary education should be delivered by local government and financed through earmarked grants or should simply be delivered directly by the field administration of central government ministries are issues for which there are no universal answers. What does appear evident is that the various pieces of the inter-

BOX 4.4 COORDINATING REFORM
IN TRANSITION ECONOMIES

A number of features of the transition economies make the establishment of appropriate intergovernmental relations particularly complex but also particularly significant for meeting national economic and social objectives; they also illustrate the importance of appropriate sequencing and coordination in the reform process.

■ Because many local governments are owners of commercial and industrial enterprises, they have an important role to play as either supporters of, or impediments to, privatization. But privatization has a number of ramifications for local governments. Among others, their finances may still rely heavily on profits from the enterprises they own. Local governments are likely to be obliged to take on important, but often unprofitable social activities—running nurseries, housing, schools, and so on—that are "spun-off" as privatization proceeds.

■ Historically, state enterprises financed many expenditures that would be shouldered by the public sector in market economies (for example, schools, hospitals, roads, and sanitation). As enterprises seek to become more competitive, they will increasingly leave these expenditures to government, in many cases at the subnational level. Coordination at different levels of government will be needed to ensure an orderly transition and adequate funding arrangements, especially for expenditures of national importance.

governmental relationship have to fit together. Little is gained by granting local political autonomy if elected officials have no discretion over expenditure or revenue levels. There is little benefit in establishing a credit-based system for infrastructure financing if local governments do not have the means to be creditworthy.

The importance of synchronizing the various parts of the intergovernmental relationship becomes increasingly evident in countries that are undergoing political decentralization. Among these, the transition economies are an especially complex case (see box 4.4). The political impetus behind decentralization has prompted central governments to make political concessions. But granting local elections is a step that can be taken quickly. What is slow and difficult is the working through of new regulatory relationships between central government and local government, the transfer of central government assets (and staff), and the conversion of what were once annual budgetary transfers within a central government into inter-

■ In a number of countries responsibility for the social safety net has been transferred to subnational governments, many of which are not adequately funded to take them on. Where the safety net is critical to the success of the transition and therefore a national policy objective, it is not clear that local governments can or should finance the safety net, even though, being closer to the local population, they may have a comparative advantage in administration.

■ User charges are typically far below costs for many locally delivered services. For subnational governments, adjusting these prices is essential for efficiency and enhancing local revenues. Doing so, however, often implies major changes in the cost of living, and if not properly coordinated with other reforms, could involve unpopular distributional shifts. The social responsibilities of local governments, as mentioned above, add to the complexity and sensitivity of addressing cost-recovery issues.

■ In the transition economies, fiscal decentralization is taking place simultaneously with national-level tax reforms, in circumstances where tax yields are erratic and difficult to predict. In such reforms, the fiscal needs of subnational governments should be taken into consideration. At the same time, central governments face a highly constrained macroeconomic situation and are seeking opportunities to compress outlays. However, reducing local resources or shifting responsibilities to local governments without adequate finance is problematic given their important social functions.

governmental transfers that are transparent and predictable. Such data as exist suggest that problems of synchronization are widespread in countries undergoing decentralization. In Eastern Europe, expenditure responsibilities were left to local governments before a workable structure of intergovernmental transfers was put in place. In Latin America, revenues were decentralized ahead of functional responsibilities. And in Africa, political autonomy was granted before either expenditure responsibilities or revenues were decentralized.

CHAPTER FIVE

Implications for the World Bank

In light of the foregoing, this book supports a change in the World Bank's approach to municipal development that is already evident in some Bank-assisted operations. Chapter 2 presented the lessons learned from municipal institution-building components in past urban projects. The discussion demonstrated that what can be achieved by working primarily within these organizations is limited. Chapter 3 then examined some of the systemwide constraints these organizations face, while chapter 4 outlined the directions for reform of these systems. The change of approach involves a shift toward more active support, as appropriate in different country contexts, of systemwide reform to increase the efficiency and responsiveness of the public sector in the delivery of urban services, coupled with complementary efforts, as necessary, at the level of organizations. The Bank will operationalize this approach more broadly, which will involve change in both how and by whom this issue is treated in the Bank. Its interventions must address a broad set of factors: the linkage of functional responsibilities to specific units of government, the correspondence between the assignment of expenditure responsibilities and the assignment of revenue, and the balance between central regulation and local feedback in the structure of accountability.

Wider Implications

Changing the relationship between central and local government has implications for sectors outside of those the Bank has traditionally defined as urban. As governments decentralize, the sectoral consequences of inter-governmental relations extend to primary education, health, transport, and water supply, to public security, and to environmental protection—to virtually any activity performed by the public sector. Changes in the structure of inter-governmental relations can also have distributional implications, bankrupting or strengthening the system of direct transfers and transfers in kind to poor populations. They may also have adverse fiscal implications (see box 5.1).

The multisectoral, distributional, and fiscal dimensions of this issue suggest the need for a cross-sectoral response from the Bank. The Bank typically assigns urban (and nonurban) infrastructure issues to the infra-structure divisions and assigns social services to human resources divi-sions, while addressing national fiscal, distributional, and general public sector management issues in country operations divisions. Increasingly, there are efforts to integrate the traditional macroeconomic economywide concerns with analysis of intergovernmental relations. A high level of effort has been exerted in some regions (Russia and Eastern Europe, parts of Latin America), resulting in very relevant analysis. This kind of country economic work could usefully be expanded. Work done in the Latin America and the Caribbean region also suggests that more cross-sectoral coordina-tion can be effective in addressing the intergovernmental institutional re-form agenda. The country departments for Mexico and Argentina, for example, took measures to achieve consistency in Bank policy messages and operational approach as intergovernmental issues were taken up more actively in these countries (see box 5.2).

Country Strategies

The review of experience suggests the need for a country strategy on institutional arrangements for local service delivery (including inter-governmental relations)—one that would be applied consistently in the Bank's dialog with national governments on macroeconomic and distribu-tional issues and in the range of sectors, both social and infrastructure, in which projects rely on local implementation capacity for success. Based on an analysis of the present structure of the public sector, the country strategy should attempt to define a limited number of key issues that the government and the Bank view as critical, paying particular attention to the institutional framework of urban service delivery—the clarity of func-tional responsibilities, the appropriateness of revenue assignment, and the structure of central regulation and local accountability. Such a strategy is more urgently needed in some countries than in others; those in the process of decentralization merit priority.

BOX 5.1 THE FISCAL IMPLICATIONS
OF LOCAL GOVERNMENT

Whether local government deficits have adverse national fiscal implications is not always clear. Local governments often run deficits on both current and capital accounts. Current account deficits—the excess of recurrent expenditure over own-source revenues—are often financed through central government recurrent transfers. Such intergovernmental "subsidies" are sometimes blamed for contributing to the central government's deficit. But this is not always a valid argument: to the extent that such transfers represent the central government's use of local governments as spending agents for national programs (such as welfare or social services), such transfers are no more (or less) deficit-inducing than the direct expenditures of central government ministries. Whether they induce deficits depends on how central government chooses to finance them.

Concerns over the fiscal implications of local borrowing for capital expenditure may also be misplaced. The fear that irresponsible local borrowing could lead to massive defaults fails to recognize that in developing countries, local governments' ability to borrow from nongovernmental sources is very limited. Unlike central governments, local governments lack the power to issue currency or compel saving by the private sector. As a result, their ability to borrow is constrained by their ability to attract private saving on market terms or to obtain the assistance of central government.

The fact that local government deficits require the acquiescence of central government is not, of course, a cause for complacency. Domestic politics can be such that central governments are induced to make transfers they cannot afford or to lend more to local governments than they can repay. In Brazil, for example, the growth of intergovernmental transfers does appear to contribute significantly to the deficit of the central government. The increase in revenue sharing mandated by Brazil's new constitution has not been matched by a corresponding off-loading of central government expenditure responsibilities. Only the revenue sharing has been implemented. As a result, local and state governments are engaging in what has been characterized as "irresponsible spending" rather than assuming a greater share of the government's recurrent expenditure.

Progress on the reform of intergovernmental relations should be a regular part of the discussion of country strategy, the portfolio performance review, and economic and sector work. To the extent that the Bank considers reform of intergovernmental relations to be as important to the country's development and to the performance of Bank-supported investments as

---

BOX 5.2 CROSS-SECTORAL COORDINATION IN MEXICO AND ARGENTINA

The need for cross-sectoral coordination is particularly apparent in Latin America as intergovernmental relations become an important element in the policy dialog. In Mexico, background work on both agricultural and urban projects examined the capital transfer and revenue sharing systems from their sectoral perspectives. A synthesis was needed to ensure consistent policy messages. In response, the Bank's Mexico country director has established a coordinating group, comprising staff from the agriculture, infrastructure, human resources, and country operations divisions (as well as representatives from the director's office and the regional technical department) with responsibility for coordination of substantive issues across their respective sectors.

A similar group has now been established for Argentina, bringing together staff from country operations, infrastructure, human resources, trade finance, and agriculture divisions. The task force has prepared a strategy to guide operations at the subnational level. An important feature is the application of the basic principles outlined in this review to identify issues cutting across several sectors, all of which rely on local government capacity. It also outlines options for addressing these issues in policy dialog and lending operations. Issues identified for further attention include areas of ambiguity (in both law and practice) in the functional responsibilities of central, provincial, and local governments that may lead to confusion and blur accountabilities and possible reforms in central-local fiscal relations to align financing more closely with the distribution of functional responsibilities. A particular feature of the strategy is its useful discussion of the potential for accessing private capital markets for financing subnational government investments in Argentina.

Other country departments are pursuing cross-sectoral themes using the "country team" approach.

---

price stability or an open trade regime, progress on this agenda should be accorded the same status in the country dialog as discussion of the public sector deficit or tariff policies.

This review has traced a steady process of learning in our municipal development projects. One of the important lessons learned is that the institutional arrangements for local service delivery, including intergovernmental relations, have an impact on the productivity and sustainability of projects. In some cases, problems in this area may be so severe that they affect key elements in the economywide strategy, such as privatization and poverty alleviation objectives. Thus, the structure of intergovernmental relations and progress on necessary reforms should be among the factors weighed in the determination of the sectoral composition and size of the overall program. Such a linkage will encourage a steady development of congenial policy environments for lending in the broad range of sectors that rely on local implementation capacity.

Lending

A range of lending instruments can serve as vehicles for pursuing the reform agenda in different country contexts. No one form of lending is universally superior to another. In general, progress on institutional reform is likely to be accomplished over a relatively long time frame—one that corresponds to a sequence of individual lending operations. Investment lending with strong policy content should play an important role in this context. Such sequences of projects—each representing a step forward on the institutional agenda—are already observed in urban development projects in Ghana and the Philippines, for example. This approach allows the Bank to sustain dialog and provide technical inputs over an extended period, adjusting the extent and nature of assistance to the rate of progress on reform and the changing political and economic conditions of the borrower. Achieving this requires a clearly articulated country strategy against which the contribution of each new lending operation should be evaluated. These individual operations may take a variety of forms. Financial intermediation projects working with an MCI or central municipal infrastructure fund, as in the case of the Ecuador Municipal Development Project or the Morocco First Municipal Finance Project, have been designed with substantial policy content with regard to intergovernmental transfers. These represent a promising approach.

Sectoral adjustment lending is a promising instrument for promoting fundamental change in intergovernmental relations given its clear emphasis on structural issues. However, experience thus far is very limited. In addition, the time frame of adjustment lending poses limitations for institutional reform. According to a recent review of public sector management issues in structural adjustment lending, "The short time horizons of SALs pose severe constraints on the effective implementation of public sector management reform . . . reforms through SALs are more successful when supported by specific technical assistance projects, country economic and sector work, monitoring and supervision" (Nunberg 1990). SECALs bear consideration where major reform actions can be clearly identified, and there is scope for appropriate follow-up work.

Consistent with this long-term nature of institutional change, attention to these issues should be spread more evenly over the project cycle. Addressing institutional issues, particularly those of intergovernmental relations, should start early in the project cycle, at identification. In effect, the decision to lend should be based, among other things, on the quality of the institutional environment in which the project would be implemented and the strength of borrower commitment. If the institutional environment is problematic, the project should be designed to address the key issues.

The Bank should also take greater advantage of opportunities to promote institutional reform at other stages in the project cycle—through sector work prior to appraisal and through supervision after it. Preproject sector work provides the opportunity for the Bank and the government to reach an understanding on reform outside of the time-bound environment of loan negotiations. The two recent urban projects that have had a significant impact on intergovernmental transfers—the Ecuador Municipal Development Project and the Morocco First Municipal Finance Project—reached substantial agreement on reform well before the projects were appraised. In the case of Ecuador, reforms in the transfer formula were enacted during preparation.

Building borrower ownership for structural reforms is a critical element in the process, and efforts outside direct project activities that familiarize borrowers with the issues can be quite useful, particularly in countries with limited experience with this type of institutional change. For example, soon after the Bank became active in Russia, it held a major policy seminar on managing municipal services and finance. This seminar brought together a wide range of municipal, oblast, and federal officials with practitioners from other countries.

The Bank can also promote reform during project supervision. Supervision should follow through on Bank-financed studies and the technical assistance components of projects. These components can, in fact, be designed to take advantage of intensive supervision, producing decisions rather than reports. Moreover, with the implicit understanding that future Bank lending will reflect progress on the overall institutional agenda, such discussions can be a means of reaching agreement on subsequent stages of reform; in this sense, supervision can function as sector work for the subsequent investment projects.

Research and Policy Work

This book outlines a substantial agenda for institutional reform and modifications to the Bank's approach to building local institutional capacity. It does so on the basis of a few relatively simple and robust principles. *These can be broadly summarized as rational and transparent assignment of responsibility for local service delivery, financing authority consistent with these functional assignments, and systems of accountability to local consumers of services and to the broader national concerns that are the primary responsibility of central government.* It is argued that closer adherence to these principles will lead to better urban service delivery and ultimately to more productive and livable cities. Thus, based on what is known today, there is a case for moving toward institutional arrangements that more closely fit those principles. However, this book also identifies extensive gaps in our knowledge that need urgent attention.

The Bank must focus on strengthening its understanding of the relationship between, on the one hand, good institutional arrangements as summarized in the above three principles and, on the other, the quality of urban service delivery. This book shows that for Bank-assisted projects, building institutional capacity from within is not sufficient; the incentives embodied in a system of institutional arrangements matter. Evidence from industrial countries suggests that good performance is associated with institutional arrangements, as outlined above. More systematic analysis of this basic hypothesis, and examination of the effectiveness of various measures that can be taken to improve the incentive system for urban service delivery in developing countries, are the most urgent research needs. This kind of analysis will help to establish with much more specificity than is now available what can be achieved from institutional reform and how that reform should be designed and sequenced.

Bank-supported operations are increasingly undertaken in the context of changing institutional arrangements across different levels of government, often associated with major political changes, as in the case of the former socialist economies of Latin America. The Bank must not let pass the opportunity to learn systematically from these adjustment processes—in particular, the light they shed on the impacts of different institutional arrangements on local service outcomes. Key questions for study would be to examine *how devolution of decisionmaking responsibility to lower levels of government affects key variables that we know are related to the effectiveness of local services—among others, unit cost of services, cost recovery, spending for maintenance as opposed to new investment, involvement of the private sector, and capacity to mobilize private sector financing for key infrastructure investments.*

A first step in building up the record of best practice is to gather systematically the evidence from Bank-supported projects, which would eventually offer the scope for *examining trends over time and across countries in institutional arrangements for local service delivery and their impacts in projects.* Task managers should be heavily involved in this exercise. In this way, the implicit or explicit assumptions underlying the proposed approach to institutional strengthening, and the assessments of key institutional constraints and how these are expected to be changed in the course of the projects, can be recorded and analyzed ex post. Risk factors should also be identified up front and their influence examined as implementation takes its course. Performance indicators could also be identified based, in part, on an assessment of what is supposed to be achieved through specific project interventions or related institutional reforms. Particular attention would have to be paid to examining the relative success of the variety of approaches used to improve service delivery. Although many of the elements of this process are already present in project preparation and supervision, the Bank's current capacity for institutional memory and consequent learning could be strengthened by devising a method for collecting and analyzing the data in a more structured fashion and for disseminating the lessons learned more broadly.

A second, related research question is *the impact of intergovernmental financing arrangements on local government performance.* Essentially, this would involve an extension to the developing countries of the applied fiscal federalism literature. The structure of fiscal transfers and the rules governing their distribution should be examined with regard to their impact on local service delivery performance and on meeting national objectives. It is well recognized that the financing arrangements accompanying any restructuring of responsibilities for service delivery are crucial. However, the Bank needs much more specific analysis of how the typically complex systems of transfers to lower levels of government affect the actual delivery of services. How well do "rules-based" systems function in practice in encouraging sound local financial management? Is predictability and timing of transfers more important than finely tuned revenue sharing formulas in ensuring that local governments spend money effectively? How does the structure of intergovernmental transfers affect macroeconomic performance in a more decentralized system? How can transfer systems be used effectively to address national or regional environmental and distributional concerns?

A third question with immediate operational relevance relates to *the interaction of the system of institutional incentives and capacity strengthening within institutions.* Operational experience suggests that without strong incentives for better performance, technical assistance and training do not have sustained impacts. However, the Bank needs to learn more about how to design technical assistance that reinforces good institutional incentives. In cases where there have been major changes in institutional arrangements, we should examine the needs for technical assistance that arise and the sorts of intervention that have been particularly effective. In many cases of decentralization, local governments are faced with major changes in their responsibilities and little capacity to undertake them. The Bank needs to assess better how quickly institutions can be expected to absorb these changes and what sorts of transitional arrangements have been successful.

A wide range of institutions are well placed to contribute to this research agenda. Official external aid and lending agencies and others involved in the implementation of development projects have an important role to play. This discussion has relied heavily on a review of Bank-supported operations, which revealed that factors not always recognized as crucial to their success were quite important. Similar retrospective analysis by other external aid and lending institutions of the sustainability of local institutional strengthening components in their projects would also add greatly to the understanding of the role of official assistance in the process of institutional change. Comparative analysis of this kind is of particular interest given that approaches to institution building and institutional arrangements for project implementation vary across the external aid and lending community.

The academic and research community will continue to play the dominant role in advancing the research agenda. More research along the lines described above is a necessity. The burgeoning research work in this area, up to now largely concentrated on the industrial countries, should be broadened to the operational questions that developing countries face. The research and policy units in the World Bank and other official external aid and lending institutions can play an important role in facilitating this reorientation of research work. The field of institutional analysis and institutional economics is relatively new in policy-oriented research in industrial countries. It is not surprising, then, that developing-country research capacity in this area is weak. Ongoing efforts to build capacity for research and policy analysis in developing countries should ensure that the institutional analysis agenda receives adequate attention.

Institutions charged with the development of international statistical data bases, particularly the United Nations institutions, should collaborate with key users, including the World Bank, the International Monetary Fund, and member countries to develop and collect comparable international statistics in areas related to this research agenda. Not all areas are now ripe for such an effort. However, the area of intergovernmental finances lends itself well to quantification, yet it is an area in which comparable international data in adequate detail have not yet been collected.

Notes

Chapter One: Introduction

1. Urban services are defined as water supply, sewerage, intracity roads, drainage, subsidies to urban mass transit, primary education, and health. A billion is 1,000 million; all dollars are U.S. dollars.

2. The inability of the traditional analytic framework to yield effective normative conclusions is summarized in Israel (1987).

3. In the interest of simplicity, central government is used throughout this book to denote the range of levels of government above the municipal level, for example, state, provincial, and central.

Chapter Three: A Framework for Analysis

1. In the decentralization literature, the two categories are variously referred to as "production efficiency and demand efficiency" or as efficiency and effectiveness.

2. In the standard public finance literature, responsibility for poverty alleviation is assigned to national governments (on the grounds that local attempts to address income disparities are likely to induce inefficient migration), and it is assumed that this will be achieved through progressive taxation and direct transfers to individuals by the national government, rather than through in-kind expenditures on local public services. Similarly, central governments are assigned responsibility for stabilization policy (largely on the grounds that local economies are too open to permit countercyclical measures to be implemented effectively), and it is often assumed that this function will be achieved through national fiscal and monetary policy, without employing local public service expenditures.

3. These statistics, based on the International Monetary Fund (IMF) *Government Finance Statistics Yearbook*, are at best crude indicators of the degree of

centralization in these countries (IMF 1992). As noted later in the text, they do not, for example, reflect the degree to which local expenditures are controlled by central government. Certain statistical conventions and data constraints in the IMF data also tend to understate the degree of public service decentralization in the G-5 countries and the consequent contrast between G-5 and developing-country patterns. First, the IMF data do not include the self-financed expenditures of public utilities (recording instead only tax-financed subsidies to parastatals). To the extent that local public utilities in industrial countries are largely self-financing (and those in developing countries are not), this convention would tend to understate the difference between the two groups of countries. Second, IMF data do not permit the disaggregation of government expenditure by function (except for the industrial countries and a small number of developing countries). As a result, it is not possible to identify the proportion of central government expenditure in urban service delivery. It can be surmised that such a comparison would indicate that the local share of urban service expenditure is much higher in industrial countries than in developing countries. IMF statistics do indicate, for example, that in the industrial countries, local governments account for the 40 to 60 percent of public expenditure on capital investment, which anecdotal evidence would suggest is not the case in developing countries. In the G-5 countries, central government expenditures are dominated by direct transfers to individuals—essentially social safety net expenditures—whereas in developing countries (judging from a small sample), a larger proportion of central government expenditure is devoted to capital works. If data on the aggregate expenditure on urban services (including self-financed utilities) were available for both industrial and developing countries, it can be surmised that the contrast in this indicator of decentralization would be greater than is shown by the available statistics.

4. Recent legislation has restricted, but not eliminated, the power of states to supersede local elected officials.

Chapter Four: Directions for Reform

1. There is no definitive prescription setting out the functions that should be assigned to local government, nor is there any standard practice, even among the industrial countries. This is not surprising, given the variety of forms of local government that exist. All the G-5 countries, for example, recognize more than one level of local government. In France, Germany, and Japan, the levels represent increasingly small subdivisions of the national territory as a whole. (French regions are divided into departments, which are divided into communes; German Landkreise are divided into Gemeinden; and Japanese prefectures are divided into municipalities.) In the United Kingdom and the United States (except New York and Virginia), urban governments are "islands" in a county "sea," with rural areas having only one tier of government: the county. All the G-5 countries also permit the creation of sector-specific entities of local government for the provision of

education, water supply, parks, or similar services. In the United States, 43,169 of the 82,341 units of local government are sector-specific special districts.

The public economics framework would argue that local government should be assigned responsibility for services whose impacts are confined to their jurisdictions. This would suggest that urban local governments should be assigned responsibility for residential infrastructure and secondary distribution systems (water supply, sewerage, secondary and tertiary road networks, and associated drainage, regulation of mass transit, parks, public lighting, and solid waste management), although this is not a prescription for municipal production of any of these services, but only for their provision. But local governments may also function as agents of central government and in this role may perform virtually any functional responsibility that is appropriate to the public sector.

2. Strictly speaking, fees for solid waste and sewerage should not be treated as user charges. Because public health externalities are associated with these services, it is not desirable to allow individual consumers to choose the level of services they wish to consume, based only on their individual evaluation of benefits. Because such fees can be clearly associated with the services they are financing, however, they have some of the benefit-equity attributes of user charges.

3. Thus, there is a case for maintaining constraints on the use of certain taxes that are assigned to local government. In many developing countries, the highest-yielding local taxes are those imposed on business activity. The specific form of such taxes varies: some are imposed on a single sector (such as the service tax in Brazil) or on certain types of transactions (such as the octroi in Pakistan); others extend more broadly to all industrial and commercial activity. In socialist economies, broad taxes (or profits) from public enterprises are the principal source of municipal revenue. Shanghai's profits tax and industrial and commercial taxes are, for example, largely imposed on firms owned by various levels of the public sector. Some business taxes have rudimentary assessment methods, taking the form of flat fees, to be paid by each business according to its particular sector; others employ more sophisticated methods of assessment, reflecting gross turnover or profits. Business taxes are high-yielding because they are indirect: their incidence can be hidden in the form of higher prices (or lower wages and returns to capital). But because they are indirect, they function poorly as benefit taxes: in shifting the burden forward onto consumers or backward onto labor, they also shift the burden across jurisdictional boundaries. Governments should therefore discourage the use of these taxes. Such taxes need not be abolished entirely, however, provided some limitation is placed on their use. In Chile, the maximum level of the business tax on any individual firm is limited to Ch$100,000 (Chilean pesos). In France, local governments are permitted to impose a business tax, but the rate is limited to a percentage of the property tax rate they are willing to impose.

4. Transfers can provide local government access to central government taxes with lower administrative costs. Because central governments are unconstrained by the need to tie the geographical incidence of their taxes to the location of their expen-

ditures, they can, and do, rely to a great extent on indirect taxes, and these are more cost-effective than the taxes typically assigned to local government. It is not clear, however, that on the margin the administrative costs of local benefit taxes are higher than those of central taxes.

5. Although the United States lags in this respect, the costs of primary education are increasingly being financed through transfers from state governments to local school districts.

6. The World Bank does not get involved in the political affairs of its member countries.

7. Among the countries that have recently authorized local elections for municipal offices are Colombia (1988), Nigeria (1989), Chile (1990), and the Republic of Korea, except Seoul (1991).

8. As O'Donnell, Schmitter, and Whitehead note succinctly, "The theory of liberal democracy was based on the presumption that active citizens would elect and hold accountable individual representatives who would, in turn, produce substantively superior decisions. Contemporary theories of democracy place the burden of consent on party elites and professional politicians (sporadically subject to electoral approval) who agree among themselves that they will compete among themselves in such a way that those who win greater electoral support will exercise their temporary political superiority in such a way as not to impede those who may win greater support in the future from taking office, and those who lose in the present agree to respect the contingent authority of the winners to make binding decisions, in exchange for being allowed to take office and make decisions in the future" (O'Donnell, Schmitter, and Whitehead 1986).

Bibliography

Azula, Antonio, and Emilio Duhan, eds. 1993. *Gestión urbana y cambio institucional.* Azcapotzalco, Mexico: Universidad Autónoma Metropolitana.

Bahl, Roy, and Johannes Linn. 1992. *Urban Public Finance in Developing Countries.* New York: Oxford University Press.

Bartone, Carl, Janis Bernstein, and Frederick Wright. 1990. "Investments in Solid Waste Management." Policy and Research Working Paper 405. Transportation, Water, and Urban Development Department, World Bank, Washington, D.C.

Bencheikh, Ahmed. 1991. "Modernisation de la propriété et aménagement urbain au Maroc: Entre la matrise locale et la logique du système foncier." *Villes et Développement* 1-91. Montreal.

Benjamin, R. 1976. "Local Government in Post-Industrial Britain: Studies of the British Royal Commission on Local Government." In B. Ostrom and F. Frances, eds., *Comparing Urban Service Delivery Systems.* London: Sage.

Bird, Richard, and C. Wallich. 1992. "Financing Local Government in Hungary." Policy and Research Working Paper 869. Policy Research Department, World Bank, Washington, D.C.

Bisch, Pierre-Etienne. 1993. *Décentralisation: L'âge de raison.* Paris: Publications du Moniteur.

Canadian Urban Institute. 1991. "Aspects of Local Government in Japan." Toronto, Canada.

Cheema, S., and D. Rondinelli, eds. 1983. *Decentralization and Development: Policy Implementation in Developing Countries.* Beverly Hills, Calif.: Sage.

Conseil de l'Europe. 1985. "Charte européenne de l'autonomie locale." Strasbourg: Conseil de l'Europe.

Davezies, L. 1985. *Les mécanismes financiers publics nationaux et locaux au Mali.* Au séminaire sous-régional sur les méthodes et instruments de planification urbaine et les support méthodologiques de l'urbanism opérationnel tenu a Bamako en mai 1985. Paris: Université de Paris.

————. 1989. *La redistribution interdépartementale des revenues induite par le budget de l'État 1984.* Report prepared for la DATA, OEIL, and IUP. Paris: Université de Paris XII.

Fisette, Jacques. 1990. "La décentralisation dans les pays en développement. Point de repères méthodologiques." *Villes et Développement* 10-90. Montreal.

Gunlicks, A. 1989. "Federalism and Intergovernmental Relations in West Germany, A Fortieth Year Appraisal." *Publius* 19(4).

Haddad, W., M. Conroy, R. Rinaldi, and O. Regel. 1990. "Education and Development: Evidence for New Priorities." Discussion Paper 95. World Bank, Washington, D.C.

Harris, Nigel, ed. 1992. *Cities in the 1990's, The Challenge for Developing Countries.* London: UCL Press Limited.

Heggie, I. 1991. "Improving Management and Charging Policy for Roads." Discussion Paper 92. Infrastructure and Urban Development Department, World Bank, Washington, D.C.

Herzer, Hilda, and Pedro Pirez. 1988. *Gobierno de la ciudad y crisis en la Argentina.* Buenos Aires: Grupo Editor Latino Americano.

Hirschman, A. 1970. *Exit Voice and Loyalty.* Cambridge, Mass.: Harvard University Press.

IMF (International Monetary Fund). Various years. *Government Finance Statistics Yearbook.* Washington, D.C.

Israel, Arturo. 1987. *Institutional Development.* Baltimore, Md.: Johns Hopkins University Press.

Kessides, Christine. 1993a. "Institutional Options for the Provision of Infrastructure." Discussion Paper 212. World Bank, Washington, D.C.

————. 1993b. "The Contributions of Infrastructure to Economic Development." Discussion Paper 213. World Bank, Washington, D.C.

Lee, Kyu Sik, and Alex Anas. 1992. "Impacts of Infrastructure Deficiencies on Nigerian Manufacturing: Private Alternatives and Policy Options." Discussion Paper 98. Infrastructure and Urban Development Department, World Bank, Washington D.C.

Legorreta, Jorge, and Angeles Flores. 1989. *Transporte y contaminación en la Ciudad de México.* Mexico City: Centro de Ecodesarrollo.

Lowder, S. 1986. *Inside Third World Cities.* London: Croom and Helm.

Marin, J., and others. 1985. "Le budget communal: Services publics, fiscalité, taxes locales, dotations globales, comptes, choix budgétaires." Syros.

Mathews, Georges, and Luc-Norman Tellier. 1990. "Prévoire l'ampleur, le rythme et la localisation de l'urbanisation dans le tiers monde, et particulièrement en Afrique." Villes et Développement 4-90. Montreal.

Musgrave, R., and P. Musgrave. 1984. *Public Finance in Theory and Practice.* New York: McGraw-Hill.

Nunberg, B. 1990. *Public Sector Management Issues in Structural Adjustment Lending.* Discussion Paper 99. Washington, D.C.: World Bank.

O'Donnell, G., P. Schmitter, and L. Whitehead. 1986. *Transitions from Authoritarian Rule.* Baltimore, Md.: Johns Hopkins University Press.

OECD (Organisation for Economic Co-operation and Development). 1991. "Urban Infrastructure: Finance and Management." Paris.

Ostrom, Eleanor, L. Schroeder, and S. Wynne. 1992. *Institutional Incentives and Sustainable Development*. Boulder, Colo.: Westview Press.

Over, M. 1991. *Economics for Health Sector Analysis: Concepts and Cases*. EDI Technical Materials. Washington, D.C.: World Bank.

Pirez, Petro. 1991. *Municipio, necesidades socialies y política local*. Buenos Aires: Grupo Editor Latino Americano S.R.L.

Prud'homme, R. 1994. "On the Dangers of Decentralization." Policy and Research Working Paper 1252. Transportation, Water, and Urban Development Department, World Bank, Washington, D.C.

Rondinelli, D. 1990. *Decentralizing Urban Development Programs: A Framework for Analyzing Policy Options*. Washington, D.C.: U.S. Agency for International Development, Office of Housing.

Salmi, Mustapha. 1990. "Le financement de la décentralisation au Maroc: De la multitude des réformes au poids des structures." *Villes et Développement* 9-90. Montreal.

Serageldin, Ismail. 1994. *Water Supply, Sanitation, and Environmental Sustainability: The Financing Challenge*. Washington, D.C.: World Bank.

Shah, A. 1991. *The New Fiscal Federalism in Brazil*. Discussion Paper 124. World Bank, Washington, D.C.

Sharpe, L. J. 1979. *Decentralist Trends in Western Democracies*. Beverly Hills, Calif.: Sage.

Silverman, Jerry. 1992. *Public Sector Decentralization: Economic Policy and Sector Investment Programs*. Technical Paper 188. World Bank, Washington, D.C.

Stren, Richard E., and Rodney R. White, eds. 1989. *African Cities in Crisis, Managing Rapid Urban Growth*. Boulder, Colo.: Westview Press.

United Nations, Department of Economic and Social Information and Policy Analysis. 1993. *World Urbanization Prospects: 1992 Revision*. New York: United Nations.

United Nations Centre for Human Settlements. 1993a. "Financing Human Settlements Development and Management in Developing Countries: A Comparative Overview of Case Studes." Nairobi.

———. 1993b. "The Management of Human Settlements: The Municipal Level." Nairobi.

U.S. Agency for International Development, Office of Housing and Urban Programs. 1992. "Final Report on Local Credit Finance: Observational Study Program in the United States." Washington, D.C.

Weber, Max. 1964. *The Theory of Social and Economic Organization*. New York: Free Press.

Winkler, Don. 1991. "Decentralization in Education: An Economic Perspective." PRE Working Paper 143. Population and Human Resources Department, World Bank, Washington, D.C.

World Bank. 1983. *Learning by Doing: World Bank Lending for Urban Development, 1972–1982*. Washington, D.C.

———. 1990. *Primary Education*. A World Bank Policy Paper. Washington, D.C.

————. 1991. *Urban Policy and Economic Development: An Agenda for the 1990s.* Washington, D.C.

————. 1992. *World Development Report 1992: Development and the Environment.* New York: Oxford University Press.

————. 1993a. *Housing: Enabling Markets to Work.* Washington, D.C.

————. 1993b. *World Development Report 1993: Investing in Health.* New York: Oxford University Press.

————. 1994. *World Development Report 1994: Infrastructure for Development.* New York: Oxford University Press.